Secularism and Its Ambiguities

The Natalie Zemon Davis Annual Lecture Series
at Central European University, Budapest

Series Editor: Gábor Klaniczay

Secularism and Its Ambiguities

Four Case Studies

Carlo Ginzburg

Central European University Press

Budapest–Vienna–New York

Published in 2023 by

CENTRAL EUROPEAN UNIVERSITY PRESS
Nádor utca 9, H-1051 Budapest, Hungary
Tel: +36-1-327-3138 or 327-3000
E-mail: *ceupress@press.ceu.edu*
Website: *www.ceupress.com*

ISBN 978-963-386-641-2 (paperback)
ISBN 978-963-386-642-9 (ebook)
ISSN 1996-1197

A CIP record for this title is available from the Library of Congress.

Table of Contents

Foreword   *vii*

Chapter One
Hobbes's Invisible Target: On the Reception
    of La Boétie's *La servitude volontaire*   *1*

Chapter Two
Texts, Images, Reproductions:
    On the Shoulders of Walter Benjamin   *15*

Chapter Three
Sacred Sociology: A Few Reflections
    on the *Collège de Sociologie*   *41*

Chapter Four
Fake News?   *69*

Notes   *97*

Index   *131*

Foreword

Is the world we inhabit secular or religious—or both? Obviously, the answer depends on the place we inhabit, on the social environment we belong to, and also on the different meanings attached to the word "secularism." But there is no doubt that the relationship between secularism and religion—punctuated by tensions, contentions, and hybridizations—is full of ambiguities. The aim of these lectures is to contribute, through four case studies, to a better (and badly needed) understanding of these issues.

These lectures (partly different from the ones I delivered at CEU in 2019*) are a small, inadequate homage to an extraordinary historian, Natalie Zemon Davis: a friend from whom I have learned much, and with

---

* The text of the third and fourth lectures has been revised. The first and second lectures are new.

whom I have engaged in an intense dialogue over the years. Thank you, dear Natalie.

In admiration and gratitude,
Carlo
Bologna, September 2022

Chapter One

Hobbes's Invisible Target
On the Reception of La Boétie's
La servitude volontaire[1]

1. At the beginning of his essay "De l'amitié" ("On Friendship," I, 28) Montaigne recalled reading *La servitude volontaire*, later appropriately renamed *Le contr'un*, before meeting its author, Étienne La Boétie.[2] That essay, which La Boétie had written in his early youth, when he was sixteen or eighteen, "against tyrants in honour of freedom," paved the way for a friendship which Montaigne condensed in a few unforgettable words: "if you press me to say why I loved him, I feel that it cannot be expressed except by replying: 'Because it was him; because it was me.'"[3]

After La Boétie's early death, Montaigne began to publish his sonnets, a satire, and his translations of Xenophon and Plutarch; however, he refrained from publishing *La servitude volontaire*, which in the meantime had been published along with some Calvinist texts. Montaigne justified his decision arguing that the subject of *La servitude volontaire* "was treated by

1

him [La Boétie] in his childhood purely as an exercise; it is a common place theme (*sujet vulgaire et tracassé*), pawed over in hundreds and hundreds of books. I have no doubts that he believed what he wrote, for he was too conscientious to tell untruths even in a light-hearted work."[4]

2. Did Montaigne believe what he wrote about *La servitude volontaire*? Probably not. The essay's paradoxical title echoed ancient and contemporary examples (Plato, Ariosto) as well as, more specifically, the expression "servitus voluntaria," used by Livy and Seneca in a negative context; nevertheless, the argument put forward by La Boétie was absolutely unconventional.[5] Nobody had ever suggested 1) that what makes tyranny possible is a voluntary decision, shared (with few exceptions) by everyone, to renounce natural equality by turning oneself into a slave; and 2) that such a voluntary decision, once revoked, would lead to the immediate destruction of tyranny. In all likelihood, Montaigne did not want to be associated with his friend's bold argument.[6]

In 1976, a critical edition of the most reliable transcription of *La servitude volontaire* was introduced by a series of samples exhibiting its long-term reception, from La Mennais to Simone Weil; two essays followed, by Pierre Clastres and Claude Lefort.[7] A close analysis

2

of one link in this chain of readings will pave the way for some unexpected conclusions.

3. In their introduction to the critical edition of *La servitude volontaire* Miguel Abensour and Marcel Gauchet remarked that according to Pierre Leroux (1797–1871),

> La Boétie is the anti-Hobbes, the one who, in his refusal of the State, deconstructs in advance all the justifications that *Leviathan* will seek to use and who, pointing to an indeterminate beyond of domination, indicates the limits of the theorists who initially posit the necessity of the State.[8]

This remark, absent in Leroux's text included in the volume mentioned above,[9] will be easily found in its original publication, *Revue sociale, ou solution pacifique du problème du prolétariat.*[10] Here is Leroux's argument:

> The antithesis of La Boétie's *Contr'un* is Thomas Hobbes' *Elemens philosophiques du citoyen*, in which the foundations of civil society are discovered.
> Hobbes was fifty-eight years old when he published this book in Paris in 1646 [*recte*, 1642, Latin version; 1649, French translation]. He had almost always lived in France [!], he was well versed in our literature; how could he not have known La Boé-

3

tie's opuscule? Would he not have read Montaigne's essays? This is unlikely. We shall see that Hobbes, that great defender of the despotic and monarchical *One,* must have read the *Contr'un.* All his dogmatism is only the counterpart to the generous but impotent protest of *the sixteen-year-old boy* speaking in the name of sentiment, and *to the honour of liberty against tyrants.*[11]

The possibility that Hobbes read La Boétie's *La servitude volontaire* had been raised a few years ago, but was immediately dismissed as "a matter of only anecdotal interest."[12] Pierre Leroux's suggestion has been ignored: an example (some would argue) of the inadequate recognition of this figure, partly due to his unusual mixture of philo-Judaism and left-wing anti-Semitism.[13] The author of the pages which Baudelaire judged "sublimes et touchantes," will be approached here from a very specific angle in order to understand the context in which his hypothesis concerning Hobbes and La Boétie emerged.[14]

4. In his youth Pierre Leroux belonged to the so called "Saint-Simonian school": a group which developed the intellectual and political legacy of Claude-Henri de Saint-Simon. In 1825 (the year of Saint-Simon's death) a selection of his writings came out, entitled *Opinions*

4

littéraires, philosophiques et industrielles, which included the following passage:

> The French Revolution, which proclaimed the ab-
> olition of slavery on the night of August 4, a de-
> cisive night which saw the fulfilment of what Pla-
> to and Jesus Christ had begun, and which, tearing
> away the last foundation of the old social edifice,
> made it possible to lay the foundations of an entire-
> ly new one. This great and truly sublime determina-
> tion made the execution of the Gospel possible; it
> made men equal, and consequently capable, for the
> first time, of living as brothers; it enabled politics,
> which until then could only be the art of deceiving
> and oppressing, to become at last a science, fruitful,
> like all the others, in salutary results.[15]

What was anticipated here, in a nutshell, was one
of the main themes of Saint-Simon's most famous
work, originally meant to appear as a second volume
of *Opinions littéraires*, but published anonymously as
an independent book due to its political relevance:
*Nouveau Christianisme, dialogues entre un conservateur
et un novateur*.[16] Retrospectively, it would be tempt-
ing to regard it as a manifesto of secularization. Saint-
Simon justified his harsh attacks on all clerical hier-
archies, seen as mere relics of the past, pointing out

5

that the French Revolution's abolition of slavery had fulfilled the Christian message, turning the equality of human beings into a reality. But the reception of *Nouveau Christianisme* shows the ambiguities of secularization: Olinde Rodrigues, the Jewish banker who regarded himself as the spiritual heir of Saint-Simon, republished the book in 1832 defining himself as the "chef de la religion saint-simonienne."[17]

5. La Boétie's emphasis on the natural equality of all human beings was, according to Leroux, "sentimental." Undoubtedly, he went on, Hobbes's axiom *homo homini lupus* was "false, cruel, abominable"; but La Boétie's opposite axiom, "drawn from the ideal, based on religion, embodied only so far in the minds of a few, never realized, is it true in fact?" Hobbes's axiom, he concluded, "will keep its force as long as the problem of a social organization based on equality and fraternity has not been solved."[18] Only the French Revolution effectively counteracted Hobbes's argument.

A few years later, in his *De l'égalité*, Leroux approached the topic once again: "Suppress equality and Hobbes is right .... Hobbes is the only one who knew the truth, and who dared to say it. But human equality was neither proclaimed nor even understood in any way when Hobbes wrote."[19] *Exit* La Boétie.

Strangely enough, Leroux ignored the shocking, paradoxical argument embodied in the title *La servitude volontaire*. Hobbes did not: La Boétie's text worked for him as an invisible target.

6. Leroux advanced his hypothesis starting from Sorbière's translation of Hobbes's *De cive*, entitled *Elemens philosophiques du bon citoyen. Traicté politique, où les Fondemens de la société civile sont découverts*.[20] I will start from a passage of Sorbière's translation of another work by Hobbes, *De corpore politico, or the Elements of Law*, which circulated as a manuscript in 1640, before being published in 1650: "Mais s'il arrive que le Maistre luy-mesme devienne Esclave par captivité, ou par une servitude volontaire."[21]

Here is Hobbes' text: "And if it happen, that the master himself by captivity or voluntary subjection, become servant to another."[22]

As we have pointed out, the expression "servitude volontaire" was far from obvious. Undoubtedly, both Hobbes and Sorbière were familiar with the title of La Boétie's text—and possibly with the text itself, which would have acted as a filter even vis-à-vis its Latin equivalent, "servitus voluntaria."[23] This conjecture is reinforced by another passage from *De corpore politico*, in which Hobbes rephrased La Boétie's argument without naming him:

7

And though the will of man, being not voluntary, but the beginning of voluntary actions, is not subject to deliberation and covenant; yet when a man covenanteth to subject his will to the command of another, he obligeth himself to this, that he resign his strength and means to him, whom he covenanteth to obey.

Here *La servitude volontaire* is evoked, although in an inverted form: "the beginning of voluntary actions is not subject to deliberation and covenant; *yet* [my italics] when a man covenanteth to subject his will to the command of another, he obligeth himself to this." But the outcome of this paradox is the opposite of La Boétie's tyranny:

This union so made, is that which men call nowadays, A BODY POLITICK, or civil society: and the Greeks call it πόλις, that is to say, a city; which may be defined to be a multitude of men, united as one person by a common power, for their common peace, defence, and benefit.[24]

A negative case shows the crucial role which Hobbes attributed to voluntary subjection:

Also exile perpetual, is a release of subjection, forasmuch as being out of the protection of the sovereignty that expelled him, he hath no means of subsisting but from himself. Now every man may lawfully defend himself, that hath no other defence; else there had been no necessity that *any man should enter into voluntary subjection, as they do in commonwealths* [my italics].[25]

7. In *De cive* (1642) Hobbes followed a similar trajectory, using more or less the same words: "Quamquam autem voluntas non sit voluntaria, sed tantum actionum volontariarum principium (non enim volumus velle, sed *facere*)."[26] In the next paragraph another minimal echo of La Boétie's text emerged:

Unio autem sic facta, appellatur *civitas*, sive *societas civilis*, atque etiam *persona civilis*; nam cum *una* sit omnium *voluntas*, pro *unâ personâ* habenda est; et nomine *uno* ab omnibus hominibus particularibus distinguenda et dignoscenda, habens iura sua, et res sibi proprias.[27]

Hobbes's phrase, "by the word *one*," with "one" emphasized in the original Latin, "et nomine *uno*," is worth comparing to La Boétie's utterance "enchantés et charmés par le nom seul d'un," that is, "enchanted and charmed by the name of *one* alone" (*Le discours de la servitude volontaire ou le Contr'un*).[28] The conver-

9

gence is evident—but the divergence between the two perspectives is evident as well. La Boétie had written that if voluntary servitude towards one man involved one million cities "this is not due to cowardice" ("cela n'est pas couardise").[29] Hobbes argued the opposite: "The cause in general, which moveth a man to become subject to another is … the fear of not otherwise preserving himself."[30] "Fear" was a fundamental notion of Hobbes's thought. Nevertheless, La Boétie remained for him a silent interlocutor—and a challenge.

8. Sorbière's translation, usually quite faithful, condensed the aforementioned passage of *De cive*, while introducing a few words which were absent in the original: "le corps d'un Estat," "l'Estat peut estre consideré comme si ce n'estoit qu'une seule teste." Was such a divergence inspired by Hobbes? In any case, he may have approved it. In those metaphors, which took the expression "body politic" at a literal value, one can hear a faint echo of a crucial passage of La Boétie's text:

> The one who controls you so much has only two eyes, has only two hands, has only one body, and has nothing other than what the least man of the great and infinite number of your cities has, except the advantage that you give him to destroy you. Where did he get so many eyes from which he hopes,

if you do not give him them? How can he have so many hands to smash you, if he does not take them from you? The feet of which he treads on your cities, where do they come from, if they are not your own? How can he have any power over you, except through you?[31]

We can imagine Hobbes reflecting on this passage over and over, along the years. Finally, it must have converged in his mind with another passage from the same section:

And from so many indignities that even the beasts would not feel them, or would not endure them, you could free yourselves from them if you tried, not to free yourselves from them, but only to want to do so. Be resolved not to serve anymore, and you are free; I do not want you to dust it or shake it; but only do not support it anymore, and you will see it like a great colossus whose base has been removed, from its very weight melt down and break.[32]

The outcome of this long reflection was the front page of *Leviathan* (figure 1).[33] La Boétie had pointed out that an act of will by those voluntary slaves would have turned them into free human beings, destroying the colossus of tyranny. Hobbes counteracted

Figure 1. The frontispiece of the book Leviathan *by Thomas Hobbes; engraving by Abraham Bosse.*

La Boétie's argument by incorporating those subjects into a unique entity: the colossal body of the Commonwealth.[34] The tension embodied in the notion of *Le contr'un* disappeared.

9. Hobbes's reading of La Boétie, although never analyzed in detail, may still affect the reception of *La servitude volontaire*, acting as an unconscious filter. The case of an outstanding scholar like Claude Lefort is eloquent. In his essay "Le nom d'Un," commenting upon the passage quoted above ("The one who controls you so much has only two eyes, has only two hands, has only one body"), Lefort wrote:

> To the visible body of the tyrant, which is only one among others, is attached the image of a body without equal, without replica, at the same time entirely separated from those who see it, in this way entirely related to itself, and which, all seeing, all acting, would not let anything remain outside itself. An image of detached power, overhanging the mass of the powerless, master of the existence of each and every one; but also an image of society as a whole, gathered together and possessing a single organic identity.[35]

One waits for the name of Hobbes—to no avail.

13

10. But the lasting impact of La Boétie's thought since the twentieth century is related to something else.[36] The very notion of "servitude volontaire" was associated with the masses supporting totalitarian regimes, and the text of La Boétie became a symbol of the fight for liberty.[37] In different contexts, this double association is still very much alive.

Chapter Two

Texts, Images, Reproductions On the Shoulders of Walter Benjamin[*]

I will start from the subtitle of my chapter: "On the shoulders of Walter Benjamin." The famous medieval metaphor—"dwarfs on the shoulders of giants"—is notoriously ambivalent. Undoubtedly, Walter Benjamin is a giant; the experiment I am going to set up would have been impossible without his challenging thoughts on the issues mentioned in the title of this chapter. But according to the medieval metaphor, even a dwarf such as I can take advantage of Benjamin's outstanding intellectual stature and perceive something which he apparently missed. I will refrain from imagining how Benjamin would have reacted to the work I am go-

---

[*] A preliminary version of this text was delivered online at the Italian Academy in New York. I am very grateful to Perry Anderson, David Freedberg, Eli Friedlander, and Manfred Posani Loewenstein for their critical remarks. Another version has been published in Spanish: "Textos, imágenes, reproducciones. Sobre los lombros de Walter Benjamin," *Papel Máquina*, 17 (October 2022): 29–46.

ing to deal with. A tortuous trajectory will hopefully lead me to approach his unfinished project obliquely.

I.

1. A long time ago I wrote an essay on clues in which I reflected on the distinction between texts which, in our culture, we regard as reproducible, and images (more precisely, a specific class of images) which we regard as unique. A handwritten or printed copy of Leopardi's *L'infinito* can reproduce the original text available in Leopardi's handwriting; on the contrary, a copy (or a reproduction) of a painting by Raphael will be, by definition, different from the original. How can we explain this difference? The invention of writing, first, and the invention of printing, later, spread (I argued) the notion of a text as an invisible entity: "All the elements tied to orality and gesture … were thought to be irrelevant to the text."

This led to the "progressive dematerialization of the text, which was gradually purified at every point of reference related to the senses: even though a material element is required for a text's survival, the text itself is not identified by that element."[1]

My reference to the invention of writing, first, and the invention of printing, later, shows that I regarded the distinction between reproducible texts and non-reproducible images as the outcome of a long historical trajectory. On the contrary, Étienne Gilson, the historian of medieval philosophy; Nelson Goodman, the philosopher; and René Wellek, the literary critic, regarded that distinction as based on an ontological difference.[2] The implications of the divergence between the two approaches will soon emerge.

2. When I advanced the notion of an invisible text, "purified at every point of reference related to the senses," I failed to mention Walter Benjamin's short, and extremely dense, essay *On the Mimetic Faculty*, written in 1933 and published only after his death. At the heart of it Benjamin put forward the notion of "nonsensuous similarity," whose meaning is clarified through language, since the written word "in some cases perhaps more vividly than the spoken word—illuminates, by the relation of its written form [*Schriftbild*] to the signified, the nature of nonsensuous similarity. In brief, it is nonsensuous similarity that establishes the ties not only between what is said and what is meant, but also between what is written and what is meant, and equally between the spoken and the written"—as well as, I would add, between the written and the written. Is this addition a tautology? No, it isn't, since the reproducibility of what is written implies an abstraction: the notion of an invisible ("nonsensuous") text.[3]

17

This conclusion is mine, not Benjamin's. If I am not mistaken, he came close to it. In German, words like "written form" (*Schriftbild*) and "copy" (*Nachbild*) suggest contiguity between the written word and the image (*Bild*) based on a sensible element which, through abstraction, turns (as Benjamin argued) into "nonsensuous similarity."[4] Retrospectively, the essay *On the Mimetic Faculty* looks like the generating cell of the essay *The Work of Art in the Age of Mechanical Reproduction*, whose first version was written two years after. But in this transition the intricate relationship between word and image disappeared, and a different, more circumscribed approach came to the forefront. A quick comparison between the starting sentences of the two essays is telling enough. Here is the beginning of the essay *On the Mimetic Faculty*:

"Nature produces similarities; one needs only to think of mimicry. The highest capacity for producing similarities, however, is man's."[5]

Now, compare that with the beginning of the earliest version of *Das Kunstwerk im Zeitalter seiner technischen Reproduzierbarkeit* (The Work of Art in the Age of Mechanical Reproduction): "Das Kunstwerk ist grundsätzlich immer Reproduzierbar gewesen" (The work of art has been always been fundamentally reproducible).[6]

A series of quick remarks on a series of technological inventions which affected different kinds of reproduction—xylography, lithography, photography—then introduced the topic of this, Walter Benjamin's most famous essay: the work of art (*das Kunstwerk*).[7]

3. Several years ago, driven by curiosity, I decided to make a systematic survey of the French journal *Revue des deux mondes*, from 1829 (the year of its foundation) onwards. As soon as I began to leaf through the pages of the journal, the earliest title of Benjamin's project came to my mind: *Paris, the capital of the 19th century.* I felt I was walking in Benjamin's footsteps, since he repeatedly consulted the *Revue des deux mondes* for his *Arcades Project* (*Passagen-Werk*). More importantly, even the path I was half-consciously following—the impact of mechanical reproduction on words and images—was related to Benjamin's project as well as, indirectly, to the central themes of his famous essay: the concepts of *Kunstwerk* and *Aura*.

4. One of the convolutes which constitute the *Arcades Project* is devoted to the World Exhibitions. In the earliest *exposé* of the project, written in 1935, the topic was presented in the following terms:

> World Exhibitions glorify the exchange value of the commodity. They create a framework in which its use value recedes into the background. They open

a phantasmagoria which a person enters in order to be distracted. The entertainment industry makes this easier by elevating the person to the level of the commodity.[8]

The *Arcades Project* is an unfinished project, first interrupted by the Nazi invasion of France, then by Walter Benjamin's own tragic death. The work I am going to deal with—*De l'union des arts et de l'industrie*, published in Paris in 1856—would have certainly attracted Benjamin's attention sooner or later. Its author, Léon de Laborde, was asked to write a report on the fine arts and the industries related to the fine arts, as a member of the "Commission française de l'exposition universelle de Londres."

I came across *De l'union des arts et de l'industrie* through a respectful, yet harsh criticism of it, written by Gustave Planche and published in the *Revue des deux mondes*.[9] The name of Léon de Laborde sounded unfamiliar to me, but as soon as I started to read his writings I was deeply impressed by their outstanding intellectual quality. As soon as I started to rummage around my messy library I found out that a demanding critic like Francis Haskell, in his book *History and Its Images*, had called Léon de Laborde an "authoritative pioneer," who "laid the foundations for the modern analysis and elucidation of the civilization" of fifteenth-century Burgundy. This, and other scholarly works, were the basis on which Léon de Laborde built up the two volumes of his *De l'union des arts et de l'industrie*, entitled respectively "Le passé" et "L'avenir."[10] But before analyzing this historico-political manifesto, some biographical data will prove helpful.

5. Léon, comte de Laborde was born in 1807. His grandfather, Jean-Joseph Laborde, a very successful businessman, died on the guillotine in May 1794. In his youth Léon travelled to the Orient with his father, Alexandre de Laborde, and published a book which contributed to the discovery of the ruins of Petra.[11] In 1847 Léon was appointed curator of the department of Antiquities, and later the Middle Ages and the Renaissance at the Louvre—a position he lost after the 1848 revolution. In 1854 he became director of the Imperial Archives (his sister, Valentine, was very close to the Empress Eugénie). Laborde died in 1869. From the amazing variety of topics he worked on with unfailing erudition, a recurrent theme emerges: the reproduction of texts and images, and their intricate relationship, explored through the impact of different technologies—from printing, to engraving, to lithography.[12]

At the very beginning of his *De l'union des arts et de l'industrie*, Laborde explained the meaning of the work's title, inspired by the Great Exhibition held in

21

London in 1851: "L'avenir des arts, des sciences et de l'industrie est dans leur association."[13] An unavoidably lengthy quotation will show how in his approach Laborde connected past, present and future:

> The intelligence of matters of taste is no longer a secret, a holy of holies which are kept locked by the high priests of impenetrable mysteries. Religion, literature, the sciences and the arts have been successfully concealed by some clever people who have kept people in ignorance under the pretext that the people were incapable of taking advantage of initiation and too willing to misuse it; but the progress of humanity, with the help of God, has overcome these obstacles. Christianity has vulgarized the worship of God; the printer has vulgarized literature; the true scholars have vulgarized science; industry, that is to say, the genius of the applied arts, is about to vulgarize the arts.
>
> Are we any less sincerely religious when we enter into communion with our neighbor; any less profoundly literate because we have our own print of Cicero and Virgil along with hundreds of thousands of other readers instead of possessing it in manuscript among a mere ten or twelve colleagues; any less profoundly intelligent for being more practical? And finally, will the arts lose something of their elevation by lowering its gaze upon the crowd;

will it have reduced its summit by extending its base? Certainly not.[14]

The crucial word in this passage is *"vulgariser,"* to vulgarize, popularize. Reproduction implies vulgarization, but this label has nothing derogatory in it. For Laborde, the phrase *"le christianisme a vulgarisé le culte de Dieu"* referred to the impact that Christianity had on religion, and the printing press on texts, and was comparable to the impact that industry would have on the arts. Laborde was developing the implications of a widespread viewpoint, scornfully mentioned by Alphonse Karr, the satirical writer, in 1839:

The daguerreotype [an early type of photograph] ... has been much talked about, has been much written about; I would also like to share my thoughts on the subject. I know of nothing so despicable as anything that "vulgarizes art," as they say, and which will only ever succeed in making vulgar art. A man of talent or genius rises to the level of art; art must never complacently stoop to the fool and moron. [15]

6. Karr's rejection of photography was very different from Laborde's attitude vis-à-vis reproductive tools. His remark on the relationship between Raphael and Marcantonio Raimondi was telling enough:

23

No sooner had engraving, a reproductive process admirably employed by Albert Dürer, appeared in its expressive, easy and popular aspect, than Raphael attached himself to Marcantonio and trained this pupil in the most perfect understanding of his thought, in the most skillful way of rendering his drawing. [16]

But something new, and on a much larger scale, was going to happen. Now Laborde turned himself into a prophet:

As with the debut of all the great discoveries, we have seen the of shrugging shoulders and the shaking of heads. Yesterday it was steam and the railways; today it is electricity; tomorrow it will be air locomotion; and so each day sees an idea rise up in the face of a mass objection. The Idea breaks through the clouds and fog; it (she) shines on the whole of humanity; and the short-sighted say to the unbelievers: It must be said that it is daytime. The same applies to the vulgarization of art. [17]

In this perspective, the vulgarization of art—i.e. the reproduction of unique works—was seen as the outcome of a long historical trajectory towards democracy, made possible by technological progress:

The intervention of machines, in this propaganda of art, marks an epoch and is the equivalent of a revolution; the means of reproduction is the democratic auxiliary par excellence. To challenge this is to be blind; to disregard this influence would be foolish; to not foresee the future of this association of the genius of the arts with the power of the new means of cheap production, is to be narrow of mind. The casting of bronze which multiplied the masterpieces of Phidias and the great sculptors of antiquity, had been welcomed by Greece with gratitude; the Middle Ages received as a gift from Heaven the printing press, which is mechanical writing; yesterday steam, that eloquent expression of modern society, gave its powerful arms in aid of all the products of industry imbued with the influence of the arts; today photography, or the mechanical art in ideal perfection, introduces the world to the beauty of divine and human creation. All these combined mediums have spread to the peasant's home the skillfully reproduced copy of the unique object of art and the hand-embroidered cloth which the rich man alone had possessed.[18]

A skillful reproduction of the unique object of art implies the destruction of its uniqueness. Reading *De l'union des arts et de l'industrie* more than a century later, we are bound to conclude that Laborde was aware that the age of the mechanical reproduction of works of art had begun.

II

1. To present Léon de Laborde as a precursor of Walter Benjamin would be ridiculous. I will try to do something completely different: to set up an imaginary dialogue between Benjamin, as an observer, and Laborde, as an actor, relying upon the categories put forward by Kenneth Pike—etic and emic. If Benjamin had come across *De l'union des arts et de l'industrie*, he might have regarded Laborde as a distant, challenging interlocutor. But the relationship between etic and emic inevitably paves the way to a series of Chinese boxes. Today we look at Benjamin and Laborde as observers and actors at the same time. So far, I have extracted a series of passages from Laborde's *De l'union des arts et de l'industrie*. How did he come to those conclusions?

A rather convoluted trajectory is needed to answer this question. We may start from Laborde's approach to a puzzling phenomenon, the revival of Gothic architecture:

It was in the early years of the nineteenth century that, for the first time since antiquity, and in imitation of the Romans of the decadence who made forgeries of the old Greek and Egyptian style, that the curious idea of remaking the Gothic emerged. England was the first to become enamoured with this fantasy. Although it had not ceased to build in the Gothic style, especially in the provinces, it can be said that the movement, produced at that time, had the characteristics of a reaction. Horace Walpole instigated it, as a hobby, cheerfully, and without giving it any importance. Serious works on Gothic antiquities written by the English, in our Normandy and at home, prove that from then on the great and beautiful architecture derived from antiquity no longer satisfied the tastes of the nation—that it needed a diversion, a distraction: the Gothic was served up as a national rattle.[19]

Laborde's remark on "les ouvrages sérieux sur les antiquités gothiques composés par des Anglais, dans notre Normandie et chez eux" ("serious works on Gothic antiquities written by the English, in our Normandy and at home") alluded to a series of books in which every item had been measured and drawn by Augustus Charles Pugin and his son, Augustus Welby, who would become the leading figure of the neo-Gothic movement.[20] As Kenneth Clark pointed out in commenting upon one of those works—*Specimens of*

Gothic Architecture Selected from Various Ancient Edifices in England by Pugin, published in 1821—"the earlier books of specimens, bent chiefly on showing the sublime and picturesque effects of Gothic, had avoided too great precision of detail. Pugin's book gave sections of every cusping and geometrical measured drawings of every crocket and finial reproduced. Thenceforward Walpole's dream of correct Gothic was realizable."[21]

Léon de Laborde and Augustus Welby Pugin were both members, along with several prominent figures of the European intellectual scene, of the jury of the Great London Exhibition of 1851 (Pugin died the year after). In his youth Laborde had been fascinated by the neo-Gothic movement, as we learn from a half-confession he made in a retrospective comment:

> There is no need to recount at length the return and vogue of the New Gothic. It has had its day as a trend (...) There is not a café today that would like to have a decorations of Ogive (gothic) arches, not a furniture manufacturer who would dare to make a chair with latice and pointed lancets; In Paris, I saw the last clock shaped as a Gothic cathedral rejected by the jury of the London Exhibition; I, alone, voted for its acceptance, like an old sinner who indulges in the memory of his own transgressions.

My error, however, had not been absolute, because my studies and travels had saved me from blind infatuation. From my early days I had given the Gothic its share, and it seemed to me justified, though today, I am prepared to take something back. No matter. The Gothic part seemed to me from then on to be purely archaeological. [22]

What did Laborde mean by stressing the "purely archaeological" role he ultimately assigned to Gothic architecture? The implications, both ideological and aesthetic, of this remark are made explicit in the following passage:

I therefore came to this conclusion: Byzantine, Romanesque and Gothic will be studied in the classes of the École des Beaux-Arts to the extent necessary so as to learn how to restore monuments built in these styles, as well as to give them their rightful place in the history of art; but pastiches of Byzantine, Romanesque and Gothic will not be made at any cost.

Will we be reproached for forgetting that the Gothic style is Christian architecture? Do those who repeat this nonsense want to exclude from Christianity all that has prayed under semicircular naves?[23]

2. The target of Laborde's sarcastic, rhetorical questions was Pugin and the reception of his work. Pugin's commitment to the neo-Gothic movement was notoriously associated with a form of extreme Catholicism, which was warmly acclaimed especially outside England. A reworked edition of his book *The True Principles of Christian Architecture*, translated into French as *Les vrais principes de l'architecture ogivale ou chrétienne: avec des remarques sur leur renaissance au temps actuel*, was published in Brussels in 1850. The introduction included a comment by the editors on Michelangelo's *Virgin and Child* on display in the church of Notre Dame at Bruges:

> A purely pagan figure of white marble, like that of the Notre Dame (Our Lady) in Bruges which is attributed to Michelangelo, will never produce anything no matter how beautiful a work of art it may be. There is nothing here that charms or attracts—she is more or less an imposing goddess, and that is all.[24]

For the partisans of the neo-Gothic movement the contemporary renaissance (*renaissance au temps actuel*) of the true principles of Christian architecture could lead to a rejection of the Renaissance (with a capital R) as a pagan movement. Even the young Laborde must have found this aesthetic chauvinism unbearable. Certainly, in his *De l'union des arts et de l'industrie* he reworked the idea of a contemporary renaissance into a project focusing on the idea of a *renaissance populaire*, a "popular renaissance":

> ... the French, indeed all the French, will sacrifice their last coin to flamboyant luxury as well as elegant luxury. Under the influence of these dispositions, the whole nation has been infatuated with a taste for the arts, a love of monuments, a passion for images, all of which are symptoms of a popular renaissance to which I would like to see the State contribute with all its efforts. I say popular renaissance because it is no longer (as in the eighth century, under Charlemagne, as in the thirteenth century, under Saint Louis, as in the sixteenth century, under François I, as in the seventeenth century, under Louis XIV) the renaissance of art of the French Court exclusively, but rather a renaissance just as beautiful, just as strong and more fruitful, because by descending to the streets it extends throughout the country.[25]

3. I will come back to this idea of a "popular renaissance" in a moment. But first, I would like to analyze Laborde's focus on France and his contentious dia-

logue with the French supporters of the neo-Gothic movement:

> No, they say, we do not exclude any style of Christian architecture, but we ask that we return to our national architecture in France. Ah, that is another topic. Where do we take our nationality from? As far as antiquity is concerned, the twelfth century is not that long ago; as far as territory is concerned, in the former royal domain, that is to say in five or six departments around Paris, it is very modest; and indeed, before the twelfth century, there is no Gothic, and outside these limits it is another Gothic, and beyond that, on the other side of the Loire or in half of France, it is no longer Gothic.[26]

"No, they say": who said this? The answer is easy. Laborde was aggressively addressing, without naming him, the leader of the French neo-Gothic movement, the famous architect Eugéne-Emmanuel Viollet-Leduc. In a pamphlet entitled *Du style gothique au dix-neuvième siècle* (On Gothic style in the nineteenth century), Viollet-Leduc had quoted in full (and reacted against) a document issued in 1846 by the Académie Royale des Beaux-Arts: *Considérations sur la question du savoir s'il est convenable, au XIXè siècle, de bâtir des* églises *en style gothique* (Considerations on the question of whether it is appropriate, in the nineteenth century, to build churches in the Gothic style). The *secré-taire perpetuel de l'Académie*, Desiré Raoul-Rochette, a well-known archaeologist who signed the document, had been as outspoken as possible: "faire revivre de nos jours ce qui a cessé d'exister depuis quatre siècles" (to revive today what has ceased to exist four centuries ago) was absurd. And he continued:

> But where are (...) the elements of such a similar resurrection, hitherto unheard of until now in the world of art? Where is the need for it in the conditions of present society? Where is the powerful hand that can lift up a whole nation to the point of setting it back four centuries? Where is there an example of an entire people that has broken with its present and its future to return to its past?[27]

Viollet-Leduc responded in kind:

> What is stirring and will stir a whole nation, gentlemen, is your long disdain for our monuments, which you praise today from the tip of your tongue, as if to make a distinction between opinions; it is your superb contempt for these truly national edifices, which neither the infatuation of the Renaissance with the antique, nor the pride of Louis XIV, who

rejected everything he had not built, nor the indifference of the last century, has been able to destroy either on our soil or in the memories of the people.[28]

4. Clearly, the controversy between Raoul-Rochette, *secrétaire perpetuel* of the Académie, and Viollet-Leduc touched Laborde deeply. The "popular renaissance" advanced by Laborde was not a "the renaissance of art of the French Court" as it had been in the case of similar movements in the past: *en descendant dans la rue, elle s'étend à tout le pays* (by taking to the streets, it extends to the whole country). As you may recall, Laborde argued that "the intervention of machines, in this propaganda of art, mark an epoch and is the equivalent of a revolution; the means of reproduction is the democratic auxiliary par excellence." He emphatically praised them all, up to the most recent—photography:

> today photography, or the mechanical art in ideal perfection, introduces the world to the beauty of divine and human creation. All these combined mediums have spread to the peasant's home the skillfully reproduced copy of the unique object of art and the hand-embroidered cloth which the rich man alone had possessed.[29]

But according to Laborde the disappearance of unique objects of art, due to old and new technologies, was part of a larger transformation of society:

> The face of society is changing; she is opening up to an indefinite future of democratic association and popular centralization which places the interests of the community and the enjoyment of pleasures within the reach of all: in politics, the deliberative assemblies and their vast audiences; in industry, competitions of all kinds and universal exhibitions; in science, the great amphitheaters of public courts open to workers, the great halls of museums and libraries; for the army, covered spaces where whole regiments of infantry and cavalry are maneuvered; for society, the great clubs, the grand cafés; for pleasure, the day theatres, the circuses, the stadiums; for the needs of the cities, the railway stations, the halls and markets, the streets themselves covered and glazed: such is the demand of well-being![30]

Everything changes, including "the streets themselves covered and glazed," *les rues elles-mêmes couvertes et vitrées*. Laborde's Paris is already, in a sense, Walter Benjamin's Paris, displaying its *passages*.

35

III.

The absence of references to Laborde's *De l'union des arts et de l'industrie* in the notes assembled for the *Passagen-Werk* is partially filled by a series of remarks on the Flemish painter Antoine Wiertz: the target of some scornful remarks by Baudelaire duly mentioned by Benjamin, who identified him as an example of "the confrontation between art and technology."[31] In an article published in the journal *La Nation* in June 1855, and then included in his posthumous *Oeuvres littéraires* (1870), Wiertz praised the invention of photography in emphatic terms. Benjamin quoted a long passage from his article, introducing it as "a prophecy from the year 1855":

> In recent years, a machine was born, the honor of our time, which astonishes our thoughts and frightens our eyes every day.
>
> This machine, within a century, will be the brush, the palette, the colors, the skill, the habit, the patience, the glance, the touch, the paste, the glaze, the string, the model, the finish, and the rendering.
>
> Within a century, there will be no more master painter: there will only be architects, painters, in the full sense of the word.

Let no one think that the daguerreotype kills art. No, it kills the work of patience, it pays tribute to the work of thought.

When the daguerreotype, this giant child, has reached the age of maturity, when all its strength and power have developed, then the genius of art will suddenly put his hand on its collar and cry out: "Mine! You are mine now! We will work together."[32]

Wiertz's article and *De l'union des arts et de l'industrie* were published nearly simultaneously: the former in June 1855, the latter in 1856. Laborde must have read Wiertz's article while he was correcting the proofs of his two-volume, thousand-page-long work. Undoubtedly, the relationship between photography and painting had been in the air for several decades. What was missing in Wiertz's enthusiastic praise of photography was the political dimension of reproduction as a general phenomenon, pointing (as Laborde stressed) at "an indefinite future of democratic association and popular centralization." Behind those vague words, Benjamin would have recognized the Second Empire's distortion of democracy, based on plebiscites. But when we read Laborde's remark "the means of reproduction is the democratic auxiliary par excellence," we inevitably recall another book which Benjamin never mentioned: Maurice Joly's *Dialogue aux enfers entre Machiavel et Montesquieu* (Dialogue in Hell between Machiavelli and Montesquieu) published anonymously in Brussels in 1864, and then notoriously plagiarized by the *Protocols of the Elders of Zion.*[33] But in Joly's extraordinary *Dialogue* there is much more than that. Its subtitle, *La politique de Machiavel au XIXe siècle*, seems today utterly inadequate: throughout the twentieth century Joly's Machiavelli has been read as a prophet of contemporary dictatorships. His bitter, sarcastic, paradoxical voice remains, for a reader of the new millennium, profoundly disturbing. Joly's emphasis on the manipulation of the masses through the press can be translated into other technologies based on reproduction, from the cinema (Walter Benjamin) to the Internet.

2. We don't know whether Léon de Laborde ever read Joly's *Dialogue aux enfers*. Apparently Laborde's and Joly's images of society were as distant as possible. But even in the case of *De l'union des arts et de l'industrie* we might speak (echoing Walter Benjamin) of "a prophecy from the year 1856." Laborde's *renaissance populaire*, i.e. "an indefinite future of democratic association and popular centralization" was based on the multiplication of objects of all kinds generated by the new technologies. All this evokes the kind of consumer society we are now all familiar with.

Laborde identified technological progress (and capitalism) with progress altogether. But on at least one occasion a darker tone suddenly emerged:

Ten years ago, every wood engraver wrote his name in letters at the bottom of an unimportant work; today, leaf through the newspapers and the Illustrated Books, the *Magasin pittoresque*, the *Illustration*, the *Musée des Familles*, and other cheap picturesque publications, you will no longer find a name at the bottom of the remarkable engravings in all these publications. Wood engraving is still an art; but everyone feels that an interpretation, even a perfect one, a facsimile, even an exact one, of another's work, is no more meritorious than copying a letter well; and the Ministry's expeditionary does not put his name at the bottom of his copy.[34]

To compare an engraving to the copy of a letter implied in both cases a definite assumption: what I have called an "invisible text," which extended from text to images. According to Antoine Wiertz, photography would have emancipated painting from its materiality, turning it into a "cosa mentale"; an argument which ended (without mentioning Leonardo) with the words, "Intelligence humaine, marche toujours! va, marche!"[35] In the same spirit, Charles Blanc had hailed with enthusiasm the photographic reproductions of Raphael's drawings: "What an admirable thing! The star that had secretly illuminated the genius masterpieces, today popularizes them by crossing them with its gaze. The democracy of beauty comes to us from the sun!"[36]

3. Needless to say, there were dissenting voices. An official *Rapport* was charged to comment upon Laborde's *De l'union des arts et de l'industrie.* The author of the *Rapport,* the well-known musician Jacques Fromental Halévy, unhesitatingly wrote:

> In particular, he [Laborde] endeavors to demonstrate that art must cease to be a purely aristocratic enjoyment, that it must, on the contrary, spread and be popularized; but, in order to do so, it needs to be associated with industry [...] In our opinion, this extreme dissemination, this "vulgarization," would bring about an inevitable and certain result: the absorption of art into industry...[37]

These words were written nearly two centuries ago. Today, the uniqueness of images—Walter Benjamin's aura—is being threatened more and more. To turn them into immaterial entities (NFTs, non-fungible tokens) would amount to a great historical loss.[38] Is this trajectory irreversible? Nobody knows.

Chapter Three

Sacred Sociology
A Few Reflections on the
Collège de Sociologie

1. Secularism is often identified with a rejection, or at least a distantiation, from the sacred. But if we assume that secularism also appropriates and reworks the sacred, its ambiguities will come to the forefront.[1] As we will see, both definitions imply a confrontation with Voltaire's thought.

In the eighteenth century Voltaire's motto "écrasez l'infâme," "crush the infamous thing"—i. e. religious, and especially Catholic, fanaticism—became the rallying cry in an anticlerical battle all over Europe. The fight for toleration and reason was bound to involve restraining (and possibly rolling back) the intrusion of the sacred in the social and political spheres. Voltaire fought under the banner of reason his entire life, but his mood changed along the way. His youthful euphoria was superseded by a gloomier attitude. As he realized after the Lisbon earthquake of 1755—a turning point in his intellectual and emotional life—hu-

41

man societies are frail entities, which Nature can easily destroy. Natural disasters and human cruelty make a mockery of cosmic optimism, as Voltaire argued in *Candide*. But mocking Leibniz's philosophy proved to be easier than silencing the problem Leibniz had tried to confront. In 1772, when he was seventy-eight, Voltaire focused once again on evil in a harangue ("diatribe") entitled *Il faut prendre un parti, ou le principe d'action* (*We Must Take Sides; Or, the Principle of Action*).[2] The distinction between good and evil, he wrote, is a notion which could be made only by examining discrete cases as they are related to ourselves ("par rapport à nous"). But then he immediately contradicted this subjective approach, remarking that although we regard the slaughter of animals, incessantly displayed in our butcheries and in our kitchens, as a blessing, "can anything be more horrible than to feed oneself with corpses?"

In his later years Voltaire had become a vegetarian, and he often dwelt on the sufferings which men inflicted on animals.[3] But in *Il faut prendre un parti* he took a broader, more comprehensive approach. Human beings, he remarked, were not alone in their propensity to murder. Suddenly the world appeared to him as a great charnel-house, in which everyone and everything killed and was killed:

Not only do we spend our lives in murdering and then devouring what we have murdered, but all animals kill each other, driven by an irresistible passion. From the smallest insects to the rhinoceros and the elephant, earth is a single battlefield, full of ambushes, carnage, and destruction; every animal has its prey, and catches it by employing the same cleverness and fury with which the execrable spider devours the innocent fly. A flock of sheep, as they graze over a field, devour in a hour a greater population of insects than the number of men on earth.

This killing, Voltaire remarked, was part of nature's plan:

In this dreadful scene of endless murders we clearly see a plan aiming to perpetuate every species through the bloody corpses of its enemies. Those victims die only when nature has carefully provided some new ones. Everything is reborn for murder.[4]

2. I will follow the impact of this passage on two readers, first the Marquis de Sade, and second de Maistre. Sade read Voltaire, of course, and kept many volumes of Voltaire's works in his library. Echoes of Voltaire have been detected in some of Sade's writings.[5] But in the case of *Il faut prendre parti* it is not a question of

echoes: one could argue that Sade, as a writer, could never have existed without it. His implacable system is a development of Voltaire's description of nature as a chain of murders. Voltaire had used words like "victims" and "murder" with compassion, linking them to his condemnation of human carnivory. Sade, in the pamphlet *Yet Another Effort, Frenchmen, If You Would Become Republicans*, included in his *Philosophy in the Bedroom* (1795),[6] made the opposite point. Murder is a perfectly normal behavior, since in the natural world murder is everywhere:

> If Nature denies eternity to beings, it follows that their destruction is one of her laws. Now, once we observe that destruction is so useful to her that she absolutely cannot dispense with it, and that she cannot achieve her creations without drawing from the store of destruction which death prepares for her, from this moment onwards the idea of annihilation which we attach to death ceases to be real.[7]

Voltaire had extended compassion to the beasts since human beings are animals themselves. Sade used the same argument for the opposite end:

> Little animals come into being as soon as a large animal perishes, and these little animals's lives are sim-

ply one of the necessary effects brought about by the large animal's temporary sleep. Given this, will anyone dare suggest that one pleases Nature more than another?

Therefore, he went on,

In light of the certainty that the only thing we do when we give ourselves over to destroying is to effect an alteration in forms which does not extinguish life, it becomes beyond human powers to prove that there may exist anything criminal in the alleged destruction of a creature, of whatever age, sex, or species you may suppose it.[8]

3. Let us consider now the impact of Voltaire's dramatic passage on a very different work, *Les Soireés de Saint-Petersbourg* (St. Petersburg Evenings). Joseph de Maistre, the great reactionary thinker, left it unfinished; however, it was published immediately after his death, in 1821. The seventh dialogue includes an eloquent apology for war as a divine, incomprehensible phenomenon—an argument whose traces are visible at various points in Tolstoy's *War and Peace*. (The two men had met in St. Petersburg, where de Maistre, then ambassador of the king of Sardinia, lived between 1802 and 1817).[9]

In the immense sphere of living things," de Maistre writes, "the obvious rule is violence, a kind of inevitable frenzy which arms all things *in mutua funera* [in mutual deaths]. Once you leave the world of insensible substances, you find the decree of violent death written on the very frontiers of life. Even in the vegetable kingdom, this law can be perceived …. But once you enter the animal kingdom, the law suddenly becomes frighteningly obvious. A power at once hidden and palpable appears constantly occupied in bringing to light the principle of life by violent means. In each great division of the animal world, it has chosen a certain number of animals charged with devouring the others; so there are insects of prey, reptiles of prey, birds of prey, fish of prey, and quadrupeds of prey. There is not an instant of time when some living creature is not devoured by another.

Above all these numerous animal species is placed man, whose destructive hands spare no living thing; he kills to eat, he kills for clothing, he kills for adornment, he kills to attack, he kills to defend himself, he kills for instruction, he kills for amusement, he kills for the killing's sake: a proud and terrible king, he needs everything, and nothing can withstand him.

After two pages de Maistre concludes:

Thus is worked out, from maggots up to man, the universal law of the violent destruction of living beings. The whole earth, continually steeped in blood, is nothing but an immense altar on which every living thing must be sacrificed without end, without restraint, without respite until the consummation of the world, the extinction of evil, the death of death.[10]

One hears, once again, the echo of Voltaire's murderous cosmos, and yet words like "altar" or "sacrifice" suggest a different perspective. De Maistre's attitude towards Voltaire was always ambivalent. The Count, the author's mouthpiece in the *Soirées de Saint-Petersbourg*, declares himself "caught between admiration and horror" when he faces Voltaire, adding: "I sometimes dream of a statue in his honor erected by the hangman"—the figure exalted by de Maistre in a famous passage which I will quote in a moment. De Maistre was fascinated by Voltaire's lucid style and clear mind, as well as by his awareness (so rare among the *philosophes*) that evil existed as a cosmic reality. But de Maistre also regarded Voltaire as a traitor, a man who had debased his rare intellectual gifts instead of using them to defend Christian religion.[11]

47

4. In Sade and de Maistre we have, I would argue, different readings of the same passage. Different they certainly were, but were they also independent? In other words, was de Maistre's reading of Voltaire affected by Sade's?

This question indirectly raises a larger one—the possible impact of Sade's writings on de Maistre. Surprisingly, this question has never been properly addressed.[12]

I am unable to prove that de Maistre, an avid book collector and reader, owned any of Sade's works. Until some decades ago they were buried, as shameful objects, in the "enfer" or "hell" of the Bibliothèque Nationale. At the time of their first publication no respectable man (and de Maistre was extremely respectable) would have kept them in his private library. During his lifetime, and for many years after his death, printed references to Sade were rare. *The Romantic Agony*, the great book that Mario Praz, the Italian critic, dedicated to the impact of Sade on European nineteenth-century literature, is based mostly on literary parallels and conjectures.[13] Its companion piece, as yet unwritten but much desired, would be a book about the impact of Sade on nineteenth-century thought, based on the same oblique approach. In that book de Maistre should play an important role. As is well-known, this arch-reactionary did not dwell on the possibility of reviving the divine right of kings and other traditions from the pre-revolutionary past. He accepted the irreversibility of the French Revolution: from that point on, he felt, the roots of authority had to be sought in an unprecedented, and utterly secular, direction.[14] De Maistre is a post-revolutionary thinker, or more precisely, I would argue, a post-Sadean thinker. In *Yet Another Effort, Frenchmen, If You Would Become Republicans* Sade combined two quite contradictory attitudes in an attempt to push to an extreme the conquests of the French Revolution. On the one hand, in the spirit of Machiavelli's *Discourses on Livy*, he stressed the need to build a Republican ethos based on a revival of the ferocious religion of ancient Rome; on the other, he advocated a radical, and profoundly asocial, release of all drives, including the urge to kill. For Sade, the impulse to kill was dispersed throughout the body politic; for de Maistre, it was concentrated in two figures, the soldier and the hangman. De Maistre's passage on the latter—the result of an extraordinary leap of theoretical imagination—is long, but deserves to be quoted nearly in full.

The hangman, de Maistre writes,

is a species unto himself [...] A dismal sign is given; a minor judicial official comes to his house to warn him that he is needed; he leaves; he arrives at some public place packed with a dense and throbbing crowd.

A poisoner, a parricide, or a blasphemer is thrown to him; he seizes him, he stretches him on the ground, he ties him to a horizontal cross, he raises it up: then a dreadful silence falls, and nothing can be heard except the crack of bones breaking under the crossbar and the howls of the victim. He unfastens him; he carries him to a wheel: the shattered limbs interweave with the spokes; the head falls; the hair stands on end, and the mouth, open like a furnace, gives out spasmodically only a few blood-spattered words calling for death to come. He has finished: his heart flutters, but it is with joy; he congratulates himself, he says sincerely, *No one can break men on the wheel better than I.* He steps down: he stretches out his bloodstained hand, and justice throws into it from a distance a few pieces of gold which he carries through a double row of men drawing back in horror. He sits down to a meal and eats; then to bed, where he sleeps. And next day, on waking, he thinks of anything but what he did the day before. Is this a man? Yes: God receives him in his temple and permits him to pray. He is not a criminal, yet it is impossible to say, for instance, *that he is virtuous, that he is an honest man, that he is estimable,* and so on. No moral praise can be appropriate for him, since this assumes relationships with men, and he has none.

And yet all grandeur, all power, all subordination rests on the executioner: he is the horror and the bond of human association. Remove the incomprehensible agent from the world, and at that very moment order gives way to chaos, thrones topple, and society disappears.[15]

5. The contrast between the hangman's gory gestures and his lack of emotional involvement has an estranging effect which is familiar to the readers of Voltaire. But Voltaire's aim was to stress the meaninglessness of phenomena usually taken for granted—from war to religion.[16] De Maistre used estrangement in order to convey the opposite: that the hangman does not perform an act of senseless cruelty, but an act full of social meaning. To trace a boundary between humans and animals, de Maistre referred, as if by chance, to an execution:

My dog accompanies me to some public spectacle, an execution, perhaps: certainly, it sees everything that I see: the crowd, the melancholy procession, the officers of justice, the soldiers, the scaffolds, the condemned man, the executioner, in a word everything: but what does it understand of all this? It understands that which it should understand *in its quality as a dog* .... The ideas of morality, sovereignty, crime, justice, authority, and so on, which are implicit in this dismal spectacle, mean nothing to it.[17]

What the dog misses is the ritual dimension of the hangman's gestures. In describing them de Maistre used a word full of sacrificial connotations: victim. In de Maistre's vocabulary this was a highly charged word. "If only we have the strength to accept what we cannot avoid, instead of being only *patients*, we will be *victims*," he wrote, reflecting on the meaning of the French Revolution, in a suppressed section of his *Considérations sur la France* (1796).[18] He went on, discussing

> one of the most profound points of divine metaphysics … the effusion of human blood … [which] has possessed eminently in the opinion of all men [a] mysterious force …. From this comes the idea of sacrifices, an idea as old as the world; and take care to note that ferocious or stupid animals, strangers to man by their instinct, such as carnivorous animals, birds of prey, serpents, fish, etc., have never been immolated. Pythagoras cried out in vain:
>
> INNOCENT EWES, WHAT HAVE YOU MERITED?

He was not heeded, for no man has the power to uproot a natural idea. (…) So it would be too much if the innocent blood flowing today was not useful to the world. Everything has a cause and one day we will understand it. The blood of the heavenly Elizabeth [Louis XVI's sister, sent to the guillotine on May 10, 1794] was perhaps necessary to balance the Revolutionary Tribunal in the general plan, and that of Louis XVI will perhaps save France.[19]

In his later works de Maistre developed these ideas more fully, arguing that sacrifice unveils the secret of human history. In a Christian perspective the human kind finds its salvation through blood, "le salut par le sang," as de Maistre emphatically declared at the end of *Eclaircissement sur les sacrifices* (Enlightenment on Sacrifices, 1821).

6. De Maistre's shocking trajectory from Sade to Christianity had a powerful impact. In his book *Sade mon prochain* (Sade My Neighbor), Pierre Klossowski – well-known novelist, philosopher and painter, like his brother, Balthus—commented on *Les Infortunes de la Vertu*, first version of *Justine*, in the following terms:

This work already includes the traits of that anarchistic philosophy which is unfolded in the novel's later versions; however, it still presents itself as an illustration of the fundamental Christian dogma, *the transfer* (réversibilité) *of the merits of the sacrificed innocent to the advantage of the guilty*, a dogma which Joseph de Maistre will develop twenty years later in his *Evenings of St. Petersburg*. Sometime later both Sade and de Maistre will be reunited in the sensibility of their brotherly reader: Baudelaire.[20]

"De Maistre and Edgar Poe taught me to think," Baudelaire wrote in his private journal.[21] Baudelaire's poetry moved between the two poles of *réversibilité* (transfer) and *la conscience dans le mal* (awareness in evil). Other names, mostly French, could be added to this peculiar tradition, mingling Christianity and Satanism: for instance, Michel Foucault. The famous opening of *Surveiller et punir*, with its gory description of the torture and death of Damiens, the regicide, would have been inconceivable without Sade and de Maistre—more precisely, without de Maistre's reading of Sade, and Bataille's (and Klossowski's) reading of both.[22] From this textual trajectory a French anomaly emerges, behind the ideology based on the separation between Church and State.

7. The names of Pierre Klossowski and Georges Bataille immediately evoke the Collège de Sociologie.

Much has been written on this institution, which lasted only three years, from 1937 to 1939. A somewhat unexpected approach to it emerged from the tortuous trajectory I have been following. But in the chain I am reconstructing, a crucial intermediary link has yet to be mentioned: Durkheim and his disciples.

L'Année Sociologique, the journal founded by Durkheim, began publication in 1898, when France was bitterly torn by the *Affaire Dreyfus*. Both Durkheim and his nephew, Marcel Mauss, openly supported the *dreyfusard* party in the political debates of the day. But the *Affaire* also had an indirect, yet profound impact on Mauss's scientific work. On January 5, 1895 Captain Alfred Dreyfus was publicly stripped of his military insignia and demoted. Antisemitic writers like Léon Daudet, who personally witnessed the event, wrote inflammatory articles describing Dreyfus, the Jewish captain, as a traitor and a Judas.[23] Dreyfus's public demotion provides the context in which Marcel Mauss and Henri Hubert wrote their essay on sacrifice, published in the 1899 issue of *L'Année Sociologique*. After having discreetly alluded to the self-sacrificing god who appears in the religions of the most civilized populations, the two authors pointed to the function of sacrifice "even outside the symbols through which believers communicate to themselves," that is, in a purely secular

55

perspective: it "is a social function because sacrifice is related to social things."

Here Mauss and Hubert's prose slowed down; their tone became solemn:

> Those expiations and general purifications, those communions, those group consecrations, those creations of the spirits of the city either give or periodically recreate for the community, represented by its gods, that good, strong, austere, terrible character which is one of the essential features of all social entities.[24]

Sacrifice is not only a social phenomenon, it is also the stone on which societies are built. Mauss and Hubert, who referred to Jesus's sacrifice only by a periphrasis, did not mention de Maistre's *Enlightenment on Sacrifices*, a book with which they were presumably familiar. Yet Dreyfus played in Mauss and Hubert's argument, albeit at a hidden level, a role comparable to the one Louis XVI played in de Maistre's: the innocent victim of a sacrifice, which in the long run "will perhaps save France."[25]

As the British anthropologist Edward Evans-Pritchard pointed out, in their work on the sociology of religion Durkheim and his pupils, who had a Jewish rationalist upbringing, frequently referred, either explicitly or implicitly, to Catholic rituals and dogmas.[26] De Maistre's idea that religious salvation would come from blood does not seem utterly remote from the secular interpretation of sacrifice advanced by Durkheim's pupils. In answering the attack launched in 1898 by Ferdinand Brunetière against pro-Dreyfus intellectuals, Durkheim wrote that a modern industrial society needs "religion," in the sense of a "system of collective beliefs and practices that have a special authority."[27] In 1938 Hubert Bourgin, who had studied with Durkheim only to become a militant of Action Française and an outspoken antisemite, provided a respectful portrait of his former teacher, depicting him as "a hieratic figure" who had regarded the founding of sociology as a religious mission. According to Bourgin, Durkheim had hoped to provide an outlet for the religious aspirations of modern man, turning society into something comparable to an all-powerful sovereign, whose orders are just and who deserves to be loved.[28]

8. Sade, de Maistre, Durkheim and his pupils, this heterogeneous constellation inspired by Voltaire's late reflections, embodies the filter through which the Collège de Sociologie, the institution founded in 1937 by Georges Bataille, Michel Leiris, Roger Caillois, and a few other friends, approached the role of the sacred in contemporary societies.[29] Bataille's presenta-

57

tion (partially based on Caillois's notes) on "Power," Klossowski's on "The Marquis de Sade and the Revolution," and Caillois's on "The Sociology of the Executioner," all delivered between February 1938 and February 1939, show how central the Sade-de Maistre connection was for the intellectual and political project which inspired the Collège.[30] Durkheim and Mauss were present through Caillois, who was a pupil of Mauss.

In the project on "sacred sociology" fascism played an important role—although one not devoid of ambiguities, as Walter Benjamin, at that time exiled in Paris, immediately pointed out.[31] Since the thirties a number of scholars have presented Sade, de Maistre, and Durkheim as forerunners of fascism.[32] From the historian's point of view, the notion of "forerunner" has no analytic value. On the contrary, the notion of "reception" is extremely helpful. The evidence shows that neither Sade, nor de Maistre, nor Durkheim played any demonstrable role in the intellectual genealogy of fascism.

In the interventions at the Collège de Sociologie each speaker articulated a common vocabulary in a distinctive voice. Bataille stressed his allegiance to Nietzsche's philosophy, and rejected Christianity as the most radical impoverishment of human existence, even as he reworked de Maistre's central categories. During recent years, Bataille remarked, the crucified figure of Jesus had been threatened both in Germany and in Italy with "images of power that exclude any idea of tragedy, any idea of killing the king." But the Italian fasces, Bataille pointed out, had a more specific meaning than the swastika, since in ancient Rome the lictor's ax "was nothing but the instrument of beheading. Consequently, the instrument for killing subjects is what is conspicuously opposed to the image of the king who is tortured to death."[33]

Klossowski, the Catholic, made a different, even opposite point. He argued (as far as we can judge from a later version of the speech he gave at the Collège) that Sade's atheism could be used to combat atheism, and that Sade's "apology for *pure crime*" might be used to demonstrate the worthlessness of reason. This "infinitely complex, esoteric method" was, according to Klossowski, a counterpart of the exoteric method that Maistre practiced in his "sociology of original sin." Antinomianism, nihilism, and moral transgression were presented as steps to salvation; de Maistre's motto, "le salut par le sang," salvation through blood, unveiled its hidden Sadean dimension.[34]

Caillois also referred to de Maistre, expanding his reflections on the hangman and the sovereign as paradoxical pillars of social cohesiveness. The pairing, Caillois concluded, "demonstrates that there is no society so totally won over by powers of abstraction that myth and the realities giving birth to it lose all authority and power within it."[35]

9. Many years ago, in an essay which was heavily criticized, I pointed out the ambiguous attitude towards fascism shared by some founders of the Collège de Sociologie.[36] The argument was not new: Walter Benjamin, as I already said, had put forward a similar judgment about Roger Caillois's writings. The same remark could have been extended to Pierre Klossowski, who in 1936 translated into French Benjamin's essay "The Work of Art in the Age of its Reproducibility."[37] At that time Klossowski had established a close cooperation with a prominent German journalist, Friedrich Sieburg, translating four of his books into French. At least two of them—*Défense du nationalisme allemand* (1933) and *Robespierre* (1936)—can be described as works of propaganda that aimed either to make Nazi Germany appealing to French public opinion, or to interpret Robespierre's dictatorship in the light of Hitler's.[38] Under the German occupation, Sieburg, as a close associate of the ambassador Otto Abetz, was directly involved in the activities of Le Groupe Collaboration.[39] This was a different situation, naturally; nevertheless, Klossowski's close relationship with Sieburg before the war is surprising.

10. The case of Georges Bataille is different. Bataille had begun to reflect on the vitality of myth in modern industrial societies and its political implications after the February 6, 1934 attempted assault on the French parliament by the Fascist leagues. In a letter addressed to Pierre Kaan, a friend to whom he was at that time politically close, Bataille declared that he had no doubts about the "archaic and indefensible character of traditional [left-wing] positions," adding, "I am sure that a new position is possible right now." He spelled it out immediately:

> I have no doubts about the ground on which we should place ourselves: it must be the ground of fascism itself, the ground of mythology. We must stress values connected to a living nihilism, comparable to fascist ideals.[40]

Instead of a strategy based on defense, he urged a strategy based on counter-attack. Contre-Attaque was indeed the name of the small leftist group founded by Bataille in 1936. There was obviously the risk of a slippage, from competing with fascism on the same ground to echoing or imitating fascism. In a reflection written in March 1936, Bataille admitted that the language used by Contre-Attaque had been at times ambiguous. But he still insisted on his fundamental point: "The Right has been able to take advantage of the communist experience, borrowing methods from their adversaries. We are convinced that the reverse is also necessary."[41]

The projects which Bataille initiated upon the demise of Contre-Attaque—*Acéphale*, both the journal and the secret society bearing the same name, as well as the Collège de Sociologie—severed all of his residual ties to the Leftist tradition.[42] In a program for *Acéphale* which remained unpublished, Bataille invoked a "community which would generate values," among which were the assertion of the "destructive and decomposing function as an accomplishment, not as a denial of being"; the achievement of the "personal accomplishment of being" through "positive asceticism and positive individual discipline"; the achievement of "universal accomplishment of personal being in the irony of the animal world"; and the conceptualization of "perversion and crime not as separate values but as elements to be integrated into the human totality." Politics seems rather far away from this mixture of Sade, Nietzsche, and Loyola's *Spiritual Exercises*.[43] But the last point of the program suggests the opposite: "Affirming the value of violence and of willful aggression (*volonté d'agression*), insofar as they are the basis of unlimited power."[44]

Bataille's text is dated April 4, 1936; on March 7 Hitler had invaded the Rhine region. As is well known,

62

Contre-Attaque immediately circulated a tract declaring that "Hitler's antidiplomatic brutality" was preferable, and ultimately more peaceful, than "the slimy excitation of politicians and diplomats." The passage created a great uproar and the tract was subsequently revised.[45] The surrealists accused Contre-Attaque of "surfascisme," a label which the group ultimately accepted.[46]

The program's last point, which is much more explicit than the tract, unequivocally demonstrates Bataille's fascination with fascism: a point repeatedly denied by his later admirers.[47] I said fascination, not sympathy. Bataille had no sympathy for fascism, which he regarded as "the most self-enclosed form of *organization*, that is the form of human existence which is closest to eternal God": the very opposite of his Nietzschean ideal of a renewal bound to emerge from *décomposition*— a favorite word of his, typically associated with putrefaction.[48] But Bataille was bewitched by the fascist display of phallic power (after all, the latin word *fascinum* means *phallós*). His decision to put himself "on the ground of fascism itself, the ground of mythology" was not a purely tactical gesture, as Acéphale, the secret society he founded in 1936, clearly shows.

11. A sectarian dimension can be detected in nearly all artistic avant-garde groups. In the case of the sur-

realists, it was reinforced by a strong interest in esoteric traditions and the occult. The diffusion of these attitudes throughout the Parisian intellectual milieus during the thirties is illustrated by the paradoxical case of Raymond Queneau. A former surrealist, Queneau broke with Bataille, his close friend, and sarcastically criticized the Collège de Sociologie for its irrationalist attitude.[49] But in 1937-38 Queneau worked on a *Treatise of Democratic Virtues* inspired by René Guénon's esoteric ideas, as well as by de Maistre's call for a reorganization and revivification of Freemasonry.[50] It does not seem surprising that several talks given at the Collège focused on clandestine orders and secret associations.[51] But Bataille aimed at a sacred sociology, not at a sociology of the sacred; at practice, not at science only. Acéphale, the sect he founded as an esoteric counterpart to the Collège de Sociologie, was meant to be "an attempt to shift from knowledge to action," taking as a model those recent phenomena in which, as in primitive societies, myths and rituals coalesce around emotionally charged images.[52] The allusion to Fascist and Nazi rallies was clear enough. Many years later Caillois remarked that the imagination of the founders of the Collège had been fired by Alphonse de Châteaubriant's *La gerbe des forces*, a book published in 1937 which depicted Nazi Germany, its meetings and its associations—especially the SS—in the most glowing colors.[53]

(Châteaubriant was one of those homosexual intellectuals who had come under the spell of the most homophobic regime which has ever existed: a troubling topic, which George Mosse addressed in a brief essay included in his last book, *The Fascist Revolution*).[54]

According to Roger Caillois's recollections, the philosopher Alexander Kojève, whose seminar on Hegel's *Phenomenology* had a great impact on Parisian intellectuals, objected to Bataille's "sacred sociology," saying that "you put yourself in the position of a magician who would ask his sleight of hands to be persuaded of the existence of magic."[55] Bataille replied that "the sorcerer's apprentice… does not encounter any different demands than those he would have met with following the difficult path of art…. The requirements of mythological invention are simply more rigorous. They do not, as a rudimentary notion would have it, refer to some obscure faculties of collective invention."[56] What happened afterwards is known from several divergent, probably reticent accounts. Bataille thought he might reinforce the bonds among the members of the Acéphale sect by organizing a human sacrifice.[57] According to the version provided by Patrick Waldberg sixty years afterward, Bataille offered himself as a voluntary victim to three members of the sect; they refused to slaughter him. What was scripted as a tragic event ended in a farce.

12. Acéphale, as a sect, and the Collège de Sociologie shared the same founders (Bataille and Caillois) but worked at different levels. One could claim that the grotesque rituals performed within the former throw some light on the ambiguities of the latter. But the intellectual legacy of the Collège de Sociologie cannot be dismissed so lightly. The best indirect homage to it can be found in two painful, guilt-ridden letters that Marcel Mauss addressed in 1936 and 1939 to Svend Ranulf, the Danish sociologist. "One thing that, fundamentally, we never foresaw," Mauss wrote in the earlier letter, "was how many large modern societies, that have more or less emerged from the Middle Ages in other respects, could be hypnotized like Australians are by their dances, and set in motion like a children's roundabout. This return to the primitive had not been the object of our thoughts."[58]

On the contrary, that very topic had been at the center of Bataille's thoughts. Bataille developed Mauss's insights, including those concerning twentieth-century societies, but rejected his evolutionary, ultimately optimistic assumptions about human societies.[59] This divergence had deep roots. Bataille shared with both Sade and de Maistre the idea that Louis XVI's beheading, by abolishing the cosmic justification for social hierarchy, had been a turning point in history. Sade's thought experiment dealing with unrestrained violence had pushed secularization to an extreme; de Maistre replied by legitimizing authority on the basis of secular violence turned into a sacred perspective. Although, as I already pointed out, neither Sade nor de Maistre can be included in the intellectual genealogy of fascism, they did provide Bataille and his friends the intellectual instruments they needed to approach an unprecedented phenomenon: the sacred myths and rituals which imposed a new legitimacy on societies like Italy and Germany, whose foundations had been shattered by the turmoil of the First World War.

The crucial relevance of those myths and rituals for the understanding of Fascism has been cogently argued by the late George Mosse in a series of pioneering studies.[60] If I am not mistaken, none of them mentions either Bataille or the Collège de Sociologie. I suspect that historians of fascism have still to grasp the relevance of the Collège for their topic. This may be not entirely their fault. The pious attitude of Bataille's later followers has created a sacred space around the man and his work, which may have discouraged outsiders. But sacred sociology must be spoken about in a profane language—which is what I have tried to do.

Chapter Four

Fake News?

The question mark in the title of this chapter—*Fake News?*—wishes to convey a critical distance vis-à-vis a phenomenon which is too often taken for granted. Distancing ourselves may help us to approach fake news obliquely.

1. I will start from an essay by Robert Merton that has rarely been mentioned in this context: "The Self-fulfilling Prophecy," published in 1948.[1] Merton, one of the most famous sociologists of the twentieth century, defined the concept he was introducing in the following terms:

> The self-fulfilling prophecy is, in the beginning, a *false* definition of the situation evoking a new behavior which makes the originally false conception come *true*. The specious validity of the self-fulfilling prophecy perpetuates the reign of error. For the

prophet will cite the actual course of event as proof that he was right from the very beginning.[2]

Some biographical data will cast some light on the implications of this remark. Robert Merton was the son of Jewish immigrants from Eastern Europe. His original family name was Schkolnick. As a teenager, having started a career as an amateur magician, he decided to change his name to Merlin, the medieval magician (Merton was a second choice). His first name, Robert, was also in homage to a famous magician, this time a real one: Robert Houdini (originally Erich Weisz).[3] This piece of anecdotal evidence is not completely out of place here: Merton might have regarded "the self-fulfilling prophecy ... which makes the originally false conception come *true*" like a sort of magic trick, which he wanted to unveil. It may be recalled that Houdini, in the last stage of his career, was known as "the hunter of fake ghosts."

All this is not so far from the Collège de Sociologie, the topic of my previous lecture. According to Roger Caillois's recollections, Alexandre Kojève had objected to Bataille's "sacred sociology," saying that "you put yourself in the position of a magician who would ask to his sleight of hands to be persuaded of the existence of magic."[4] Bataille, who defiantly defined himself as an "apprenti sorcier," might have recalled the famous sentence put forward by Tacitus, the Roman historian:

"*fingunt simul creduntque*," "they make it up and believe in it at the same time." As Freud taught us the power of self-deception, we are now ready to accept Tacitus's bold paradox. But Merton's "prophet" is well aware that the false news he is spreading is false—until its success turns it into a truth. At the end of his essay Merton added a remark in italics: "*The self-fulfilling prophecy, whereby fears are translated into reality, operates only in the absence of deliberate institutional controls.*"[5]

Today, in the age of the Web, these remarks ring a familiar bell. I will try to explore the implications of Merton's notion of self-fulfilling prophecy in different directions, both retrospectively and prospectively. Hopefully, this will cast some unexpected light on the notion, and practice, of fake news.

2. Two of the greatest historical books written in the twentieth century were devoted to events that today we regard as untrue: Marc Bloch's *Les rois thaumaturges* (1924), translated into English as *The Royal Touch*, and Georges Lefebvre's *La grande peur de 1789* (1932), translated as *The Great Fear of 1789*. At that time Bloch and Lefebvre were both teaching in Strasbourg, the city that had become, at the end of the First World War, the symbol of victorious France.[6]

In *Les rois thaumaturges* Bloch analyzed, as the subtitle reads, "the supernatural character ascribed to the royal power especially in France and England," focusing on the virtue, attributed to legitimate kings of both countries, to heal men and women who suffered from scrofula: an illness affecting the neck glands. As a motto for his book Bloch chose a sentence from Montesquieu's *Lettres persanes*: "ce roi est un grand magicien," "this king is a great magician." The rumors concerning this supernatural capacity, Bloch argued, had been spread deliberately during the Middle Ages, both in France and in England, to reinforce royal power. The last French king to touch people suffering from scrofula was Charles X, in 1829; a detail that shows how many people, along the centuries, regarded the kings' magical powers to be true.

Many years ago I advanced a connection between *Les rois thaumaturges* and Bloch's experience as a soldier in the First World War, conveyed in the essay "Réflexions sur les fausses nouvelles de la guerre," "Reflections of a Historian on the False News of the War" (1921). Bloch approached the kings' magical power to heal people suffering from scrofula as if it were a gigantic *fausse nouvelle*, comparable to the uncontrolled fake news that circulated in the trenches.[7] I shall return to this later.

3. The healing power attributed to French and English kings, analyzed by Bloch, was fictitious. Likewise,

the conspiracy staged by French aristocrats against the peasants, which is at the center of Georges Lefebvre's *La grande peur de 1789*, was a non-event. This alleged revenge for the fall of the Bastille, never took place; however, the rumours about it generated a panic in the countryside, which triggered a sequence of real violence. "A gigantic movement, generated by false news," Franco Venturi remarked, stressing the commitment to unveil the truth, in the spirit of Voltaire, shared by both Bloch and Lefebvre.[8] Through this case study Lefebvre explored the deep attitudes of the French peasants, reacting to a wave of panic in a time of crisis, at a very early stage of the Revolution. One may recall that Merton regarded his notion of self-fulfilling prophecy as a reworking of the so-called "Thomas Theorem," advanced by the American sociologist, William Thomas: "if men define situations as real, they are real in their consequences."[9] But to assume, as Merton did, that the initial prophecy is deliberately false, implies a crucial difference.

4. In an essay devoted to "Revolutionary crowds" (1932), closely related to his book *La grande peur*, Lefebvre sharply criticized the most influential work ever written about crowds: Gustave Le Bon's *Psychologie des foules*. First published in 1895 by a polymath who never succeeded in entering academia, *Psychologie des foules*

has been reprinted many times until the present and translated into many languages. Although it is widely considered as one of the founding texts of collective psychology, its status has remained, especially in France, highly controversial.[10] It is undoubtedly an antirevolutionary book, written by a racist author.[11] In recent years Le Bon's work has been appropriated by a right-wing group called "Amis de Gustave Le Bon," which reprinted, among others, his anti-Semitic booklet *Le rôle des juifs dans la civilization*.[12] Le Bon's work has been repeatedly praised by Alain de Benoist, the "Nouvelle Droite" intellectual—an act which also has a personal component, since his paternal grandmother, Yvonne de Benoist, was Gustave Le Bon's secretary.[13]

But let us return to Georges Lefebvre, and his reading of Le Bon's *Psychologie des foules* in 1932. The main weakness of Le Bon's argument, according to Lefebvre, was a terminological and conceptual confusion between *foules* (crowds) and *masses* (masses).[14] It is worth noting that though this distinction exists in French and English (as well as in Italian), interestingly, it does not exist in German, where *Massen* means both "crowds" (informal, ephemeral human conglomerates) and "masses" (social groups).[15]

A passage from the very beginning of Le Bon's book apparently exemplifies the terminological and conceptual confusion pointed out by Lefebvre. Le Bon emphasized that his target was "the entry of the popular classes into political life—that is to say, in reality, their progressive transformation into governing classes."

Then, in a sudden shift, he went on:

Today the claims of the masses are becoming more and more sharply defined, and amount to nothing less than a determination to utterly destroy society as it now exists, with a view to making it hark back to that primitive communism which was the normal condition of all human groups before the dawn of civilization.[16]

5. Le Bon's shift from "popular classes" to "crowds" is blatant. Was it due to a conceptual confusion—or was Le Bon implicitly suggesting a political strategy aimed to counteract "the threatening invasion of socialism (*l'invasion menaçante du Socialisme*)"?[17] The use of the future tense in a solemn statement such as "The age we are entering will be a true AGE OF CROWDS" ("L'âge où nous entrons sera véritablement L'ÈRE DES FOULES") is ambiguous.[18] Far from announcing an inevitable trajectory, Le Bon was proposing a detailed argument which implicitly aimed to contribute in turning his seemingly neutral, "scientific" statement into a different reality.[19] "A knowledge of the psychology of crowds," Le Bon wrote in the in-

troduction to his book, "is today the last resource of the statesman who wishes not to govern them—that is becoming very difficult—but at any rate not to be too much governed by them."[20] But the detailed instructions advanced in *Psychologie des foules* show that its project was much more ambitious. As Emilio Gentile argued, Le Bon could be compared to the Machiavelli of the age of the masses, who aimed to teach how to control and to rule the crowds.[21]

According to Le Bon, the crowd's distinctive features are "impulsiveness, irritability, incapacity to reason, the absence of judgment and of the critical spirit, the exaggeration of the sentiments, and others besides —which are almost always observed in beings belonging to inferior forms of evolution—in women, savages, and children for instance."[22]

Crowds are weak, irrational, dominated by contagion: "a phenomenon [which] must be classed among those phenomena of a hypnotic order (*un phénomène … qu'il faut rattacher aux phénomènes d'ordre hypnotique*)."[23] Is this a description—or a suggestion? If we accept the latter alternative, we must conclude that Le Bon was implicitly arguing that the masses should be turned into crowds, relying upon "the power of the hypnotiser over the hypnotised (*le pouvoir de l'hypnotiseur sur l'hypnotisé*)."[24] This implicit reference to Charcot and his experiences at the Salpêtrière, to Bernheimer, and to the Nancy school explain why, according to Le Bon, the role of consciousness in social life was (or should be) minimal: "Visible social phenomena appear to be the result of an immense, unconscious working (*un immense travail inconscient*), that as a rule is beyond the reach of our analysis)."[25]

Le Bon's ultimate political message was clear enough: "Crowds are too much governed by unconscious considerations (*les foules sont trop régies par l'inconscient*), and too much subject in consequence to secular hereditary influences not to be extremely conservative."[26]

Therefore, crowds (including parliamentary crowds) need a "meneur," a leader, since "men forming a crowd cannot do without a master (*les hommes en foule ne sauraient se passer d'un maître*)."[27] An entire chapter entitled "The Leaders of Crowds and Their Means of Persuasion" (*Les meneurs des foules et leurs moyens de persuasion*), includes passages like this:

To make a skilful use of these resources a leader must have arrived at a comprehension, at least in an unconscious manner (*au moins d'une façon inconsciente*), of the psychology of crowds, and must know how to address them. He should be aware, in particular, of the fascinating influence of words, phrases, and images. He should possess a special description of eloquence, composed of energetic affirmations—

unburdened with proofs—and impressive images, accompanied by very summary arguments.[28]

6. In his *Group Psychology and the Analysis of the Ego* (1921), Sigmund Freud commented at length on Le Bon's *Psychologie des foules*, although he pointed out that its content was not new, since it had been anticipated by Scipio Sighele, the Italian sociologist. Moreover, Freud considered the notion of *meneur* inconsistent with Le Bon's "brilliantly executed picture" of the crowd's soul.[29] Brilliant, may be, but it is also superficial, and full of commonplaces (most of them reactionary and racist). In any case, if we read Le Bon's *Psychologie des foules* as a political act, rather than as a neutral, scientific analysis (which it is not), its reception becomes highly significant. Le Bon's book was annotated by Lenin and Kemal Atatürk, and possibly read by Hitler; Le Bon's admirers included, besides Theodore Roosevelt and Georges Clemenceau, Benito Mussolini.

7. In 1926, when interviewed by a French journalist, Mussolini said:

"I have read Le Bon's *Psychology of Crowds* innumerable times: a fundamental work—I often go back to it *even today*."[30] A passage from a speech delivered by Mussolini in Cremona, on June 19, 1923, may convey a feeble echo of what he had learned from Le Bon's book: "Io guardo nei vostri occhi, che possono guardare nei miei e interrogarmi e domando" ("I look you into your eyes, which can look into mine and question me, and I ask").

This passage was quoted, and commented on, by Curt Gutkind, the editor of a collection of essays by various authors entitled *Mussolini e il fascismo*, published in Italian and German in 1926, with an introduction by Mussolini himself. Gutkind, at that time a committed fascist, wrote:

> His gaze, with magnetic strength, captures thousands of eyes, taking them into the sphere of his will; he pierces those eyes, trying to identify himself with the soul of this or that individual, whose traits for some reason had aroused his attention. More often, however, there is a mutual magic involving two entities that cross each other: sparks spring from this crossing. One of these entities is the Mass: it feels the charm of the Man, because it knows that he is one of them, because it knows that he is its master.[31]

This kind of bombastic fascist rhetoric is well known. But its metaphors—hypnotism, magic, magnetic strength, as well as its erotic overtones—are significant, since they point to a language shared by both the observer (Gutkind) and the main actor, Mussolini himself. A few years later, in 1932, Emil Ludwig, a German Jewish journalist, published a series of conversations with Mussolini. In reading the proofs, Mussolini changed one of his remarks—"*La massa ama gli uomini forti. La massa è femmina*" (The mass loves strong men. The mass is female) into "*la massa è donna*," emphasizing the allusion to Machiavelli (*Il Principe*, ch. XXV: ("La fortuna è donna," "fortune is a woman").[32]

8. This allusion was part of a deliberate communication strategy. In April 1924, Mussolini had published in *Gerarchia*, the official journal of the Fascist party, an essay entitled "Prelude to Machiavelli."[33] In this short, cursory piece, based exclusively on *The Prince*, Mussolini insisted on Machiavelli's praise of force and contempt for human beings—a contempt he, Mussolini, not only shared but, on the basis of his experience, possibly worsened.[34]

In Emil Ludwig's conversations with Mussolini, the "teacher of dictators" (as Ludwig labeled Machiavelli) surfaced both directly and indirectly. Mussolini told his interlocutor that his own father, a Socialist blacksmith, used to read Machiavelli to his children after dinner. Invented or not, the story underlined Mussolini's appropriation of Machiavelli as part of his public image.

"You wrote once," stated Ludwig, "that the masses ought not to know, but to believe." Mussolini emphatically agreed:

> The capacity of the modern man for faith is illiminitable. When the masses are like wax in my hands, when I stir their faith, or when I mingle with them, and am almost crushed by them, I feel myself to be a part of them. All the same, there persists in me a certain feeling of aversion, like that which the modeller feels for the clay he is moulding. Does not the sculptor sometimes smash his block of marble into fragments because he cannot shape it to represent the vision he has conceived? Now and then this crude matter rebels against the creator!

And then, after a pause: "Everything turns upon one's ability to control the masses like an artist."[35]

The subtext of Mussolini's tirade was a passage from Machiavelli's *The Art of War*, suggesting a comparison—one inspired by Michelangelo's *David*) (figure 2)— between imposing a belief over the people and carving a statue from a piece of marble:

> for this form can only be stamped upon simple, rough, and independent men, not upon evil, badly governed, and foreign ones. Nor has any good

Figure 2. "David" by Michelangelo, Florence, Galleria dell'Accademia, 1501–1504

sculptor ever been found who believes that he can make as beautiful a statue from a piece of poorly blocked marble as he can from one that is rough.[36]

Obviously, Machiavelli and Mussolini lived and worked in completely different contexts. Mussolini addressed the mass, "la massa"—a new phenomenon, designated by an ambiguous word, which referred at one and the same time to both physical matter and to human beings. It was this ambiguity which paved the way for Mussolini's conclusion: "to control the masses like an artist."

"The logical outcome of fascism is an aestheticizing of political life," wrote Walter Benjamin, the German philosopher and critic, in his famous essay "The Work of Art in the Age of Its Reproducibility."[37] These words sound like a comment on the passage I just quoted from Emil Ludwig's *Conversations with Mussolini*: a book which Benjamin presumably had read in German a few years before.[38] In any case, Mussolini's self-presentation, recorded by Ludwig, was contagious. On March 12, 1933 the German satirical magazine *Kladderadatsch* published a drawing, with anti-Semitic overtones, showing Hitler, "the sculptor of Germany," in the act of molding the new German man, shaped like a statue by Arno Breker (figure 3).[39]

83

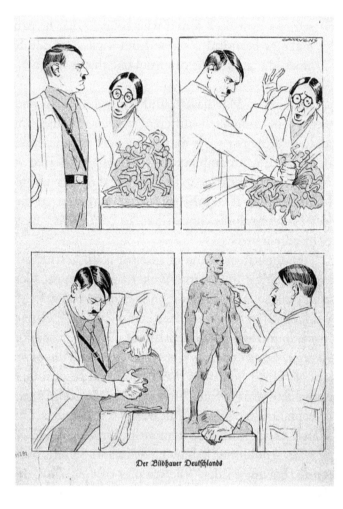

Figure 3. "The sculptor of Germany" by Oscar Garvens, published in Kladderadatsch *magazine in 1933*

But another metaphor surfaced over and over to describe the relationship between Mussolini and the crowd: his way of addressing it, fixing it in the eyes. Le Bon's remark on "the power of the hypnotizer over the hypnotized" (*le pouvoir de l'hypnotiseur sur l'hypnotisé*) echoed Gabriel Tarde, the influential sociologist, who had chosen "the example of the magnetizer" to unveil the secret of social power: "The magnetiser does not need to lie or terrorise to secure the blind belief and the passive obedience of his magnetised subject. He has prestige – that tells the story."[40]

In his *Les Transformations du pouvoir* (*The Transformations of Power*, 1899) Tarde reworked this issue in a different direction. "The feeling of joy generated by freedom," he wrote, "is a noble feeling, for sure— but not so widespread as it is usually said. In fact, for most people an irresistible pleasure is associated with obedience, credulity, and a quasi-loving submission to a master they admire." This is what, he concluded, Étienne de La Boétie (Michel de Montaigne's closest friend) said in his *Discours de la servitude volontaire* (*Discourse on Voluntary Servitude*), which was the topic of my first lecture.[41]

This unexpected reference could be read as an implicit comment on Le Bon's *Psychologie des foules*— a book which Tarde did not mention explicitly. The crowd wants to submit, and loves its master, therefore…

After two hundred pages, the reader of *Les Transformations du pouvoir* comes across a remark on the potentialities of the press that seems to unfold the implications of the passage I have just noted: "Therefore, we can safely predict that in the future we will see personifications of authority and power that will shame the greatest despots of the past, from Julius Caesar, to Louis XIV, to Napoleon." Such a statesman, Tarde continues, "will be able to realize political *and social* programs whose boldness would have terrified even Bismarck." But after having evoked this "imminent" and frightening "gigantic power" (*Pouvoir gigantesque*), Tarde declares, perhaps with some hesitation, that we should be somewhat reassured by its very dimension.[42]

9. In 1908 Umberto Boccioni, the Futurist painter, provided, unknowingly, a visual equivalent of the "gigantic power" that Gabriel Tarde felt approaching in 1899 (figure 4). In this updated version of Andrea del Verrocchio's Venetian monument to Bartolomeo Colleoni, the fifteenth century *condottiere* (figure 5), Boccioni represented a *meneur* surmounting a worshipping crowd. A few years later, in 1919, the word *meneur*, which had been used in a political sense by Hyppolite Taine and made popular by Le Bon, reappeared in an insightful, prophetic portrait of the young Mussolini, written by a top-level police functionary, Giovanni Gasti:

Figure 4. Umberto Boccioni, Folla che circonda un monumento equestre *(Crowd surrounding an equestrian monument), 1908, ink on paper (Winston Collection, Birmingham)*

Figure 5. Equestrian statue of Bartolomeo Colleoni, by Andrea del Verrocchio. Campo Santi Giovanni e Paolo, Venice

This effective and incisive writer [Mussolini], this persuasive and lively orator," Gasti wrote "could become a *condottiero*, a formidable *meneur*" (questo scrittore efficace ed incisivo, questo oratore persuasivo e vivace, potrebbe diventare un condottiero, un *meneur* temibile).[43]

Meneur, condottiero—and then duce, *Führer.* The same word, translated into different languages, conveys a momentous historical trajectory, compressed into a few years.

10. These pervasive metaphors inspired Thomas Mann's famous novella *Mario und der Zauberer, Mario and the Magician* (1929): an allegory of fascism in which a professional hypnotist, named Cipolla, subjugates the audience of an Italian seaside resort—until the young Mario kills him.[44] (The pervasive use of hypnotism, as a metaphor of fascism, could be compared to one of those shared social experiences analyzed by Michael Baxandall in his book on Quattrocento Italian painting.[45]) A distinct echo of Mann's novella may be read in the suggestion, advanced by Siegfried Kracauer in his book *From Caligari to Hitler. A Psychological History of the German Film* (1946), that Dr. Caligari, the movie character, could be regarded as a premonition of Hitler:

Caligari is a very specific premonition in the sense that he uses hypnotic power to force his will upon his tool—a technique foreshadowing, in content and purpose, that manipulation of the soul which Hitler was the first to practice on a gigantic scale. … They [the two authors of the film script, Janowitz and Mayer] must have been driven by one of those dark impulses which, stemming from the slowly foundations of a people's life, sometimes engender true visions.[46]

From Caligari to Hitler, from Gustave Le Bon to Hitler?—this trajectory would be simplistic. But the impact of a shared metaphor—the crowd leader compared to a hypnotist—leads us to the role played by propaganda in twentieth-century dictatorships. As I have said, Hitler may have read Le Bon's *Psychologie des foules* (although this is far from proven).[47] But the impact of a shared metaphor—the crowd leader compared to a hypnotist—leads us to the role played by propaganda in twentieth-century dictatorships, i.e. the context in which fake news, as an updated version of self-fulfilling prophecy, has emerged. Le Bon would have been unable to imagine this context, but is it possible to rework his arguments in the age of the Web?

This question has been raised by Carsten Stage, a Danish scholar, in an essay entitled "The Online Crowd: A Contradiction in Terms? On the Potentials of Gustave Le Bon's Crowd Psychology in an Analysis of Affective Blogging."[48] Perhaps we can reformulate the question adding one more adjective: "the lonely online crowd: a contradiction in terms?"

The answer would be "no." A crowd of consumers, as David Riesman anticipated long ago, hungry for commodities of all kinds is definitely not a contradiction in terms. We are living in an "ère des foules," an era of crowds, which share some features with the one Le Bon was both announcing, and ambiguously fighting for, as a remedy to the threat of Socialism. This lonely crowd is hungry not only for commodities but also for publicity related to commodities—compara-

Figure 6. "Your Country Needs You," recruitment poster, UK, 1914

Figure 7. Advertisement for Godfrey Phillips Cigarettes, London, c. 1910

ble to "affirmations énergiques—dégagées des preuves," mentioned by Le Bon. As I argued elsewhere, in the First World War political propaganda took its inspiration from publicity: Lord Kitchener addressing the viewer with a pointed finger echoed a poster advertising a cigarette brand (figures 6 and 7). In a chapter of *Mein Kampf* devoted to war propaganda, Adolf Hitler emphatically emphasized that the model for political propaganda should be the advertisement, i.e. a kind of communication unconcerned with truth or falsehood: "The people in their overwhelming majority are so feminine by nature and attitude that sober reasoning determines their thoughts and actions far less than emotion and feeling."[49] Once again, Hitler was echoing (either directly or indirectly) Gustave Le Bon, who had stressed, besides the feminine nature of the crowd, "the astonishing power of advertisements. When we have read a hundred, a thousand times that X's chocolate is the best, we imagine we have heard it said in many quarters, and we end by acquiring the certitude that such is the fact."[50]

A crowd ready to accept "energetic statements not accompanied by proof" will also be ready to accept fake news. But is it possible to fight against fake news?

12. At the beginning of my lecture, I evoked the context in which Marc Bloch's great book, *Les rois thaumaturges*, emerged: the circulation of *fausses nouvelles* in the First World War trenches. The debates on this topic started at the very beginning of the war, with the German invasion of Belgium. The news concerning German atrocities, and especially the murder of civil-

ians, were denounced as a falsity by the German press. In a highly significant move, the French government asked a prominent philologist, Joseph Bédier, a long-time professor at the Collège de France, to counter those accusations. Bédier, relying on a detailed analysis of notebooks scribbled by German officers, proved that the reports concerning the murder of civilians were authentic.[51]

This event can be inscribed in a long history. The political potentialities of philology had emerged a long time before—at least since Lorenzo Valla, the Italian humanist, demonstrated in 1440 that the alleged *Donation of Constantine* was a forgery.[52] According to the *Donation*, Constantine, the Roman emperor who converted to Christianity, had left one third of the Empire to the Church prior to his death. Valla disproved the authenticity of the *Donation* on the basis of some blatant textual anachronisms—a demonstration that (some dissenting voices notwithstanding) is traditionally regarded as a crucial contribution to the historical method.[53] However, as I realized some years ago, a crucial passage of Valla's text has been overlooked.[54]

The *Donation of Constantine* includes a reference to the document itself in the following terms: "Reinforcing the page of this imperial decree [the Donation] by our very own hands, we have placed it on the venerable body of the blessed Peter."

Here is Valla's comment:

When I was a boy, I remember asking someone who had written the Book of Job. When he answered, "Job himself," I asked the further question of how therefore he managed to mention his own death. This can be said of many other books, although it is not appropriate to discuss them here. For how can something that has not yet taken place be accurately told? How can the tablets include something which he admits himself occurred after the burial, so to speak, of the tablets?[55]

To the best of my knowledge, no modern commentator has paid attention to the sentence: "This can be said of many other books, although it is not appropriate to discuss them here." But its meaning, albeit implicit, is obvious. Valla was tacitly referring to the last chapter of *Deuteronomy* (34:5ff.):
"So Moses the servant of the Lord died there in the land of Moab, according to the word of the Lord..."
Even a bold writer like Valla, in the boldest of his works, did not dare to argue that Moses was not, and could not be, the author of the *Pentateuch*. Valla chose an oblique strategy—the one that Leo Strauss analyzed in his famous essay "Persecution and the Art of Writing."[56] How many readers were able to read Valla's

text between the lines, grasping its hidden reference? We shall never know. But retrospectively, we are entitled to regard Valla's allusive remark as a turning point in the long history of a secular approach to the Bible.

Allusive, but unambiguous. Its implications are self-evident. We must learn to read all kinds of texts between the lines; we must learn to disprove fake news. Digital philology has (hopefully) a future.

Notes

1 This text started as a reflection on Quentin Skinner's essay "On Neo-Roman Liberty: A Response and a Reassessment," in *Rethinking Liberty before Liberalism*, ed. Hannah Dawson and Annelien de Dijn (Cambridge: Cambridge University Press, 2022), 233–66. I am deeply grateful to Quentin Skinner for his invaluable comments and suggestions related to a previous version of this essay. The trajectory and the conclusions are mine.

2 Michel de Montaigne, *Essais*, ed. Albert Thibaudet (Paris: Bibliotheque de la Pleiade–Gallimard, 1950), 218–19: "C'est un discours auquel il [Estienne de la Boétie] donna nom LA SERVITUDE VOLONTAIRE, mais ceux qui l'ont ignoré, l'ont bien proprement depuis rebaptisé LE CONTR'UN." In this context, it will be appropriate (as Quentin Skinner pointed out to me) to mention also John Florio's translation: "It is a discourse he entitled *Voluntary servitude*, but those who have not known him, have since very properly rebaptized the same *the Against one*." M. de Montaigne, *The Essayes or Morall, Politike and Millitarie Discourses* (London: Val. Sims for Edward Blount, 1603), 90.

3 Montaigne, *Essais*, 224: "Si on me presse de dire pourquoy je l'aymois, je sens que cela ne se peut exprimer, qu'en respondant: Par ce que c'estoit luy; par ce que c'estoit moy."

4 Montaigne, *Essais*, 232. For the English translation, see: Michel de Montaigne, *The Complete Essays*, trans. M. A. Screech (London: Allen Lane, 1991), 218–19. The passage is not mentioned in Jean Starobinski's unilateral presentation of the relationship between Montaigne and La Boétie: *Montaigne en mouvement* (Paris: Gallimard, 1983), 52–86.

5 Livy, XXVII, 25, 8: "Quando Eumenes in voluntariam servitutem concessisset." (Livy, *Ab urbe condita*, XXXVII, 25, 8, pointed to me by Quentin Skinner); Seneca, *Epistulae ad Lucilium*, XLVII, 17: "Nulla servitus turpior est quam voluntaria." Both references have been ignored by Louis Delaruelle, "L'inspiration antique dans le 'Discours sur la servitude volontaire,'" *Revue d'histoire littéraire de la France* 17

(1910), 34–72, as well as by Joseph Barrère, *L'humanisme et la politique dans le Discours de la servitude volontaire* (Paris: Edouard Champion, 1923), 16–19. Both Plato (*Symposium*, translated by Louis Le Blanc) and Ariosto (*Orlando furioso*, XLV, 46) used the expressions "servitude volontaire" and "volontaria… servitude" in a positive sense.

6   On the transmission of La Boétie's text (and Montaigne's role in preserving it), see Renzo Ragghianti, *Rétablir un texte. Le* Discours de la servitude volontaire *d'Étienne La Boétie* (Florence: L.S. Olschki, 2010).

7   Étienne de La Boétie, *Le discours de la servitude volontaire*, ed. Pierre Léonard (Paris: Petite bibliothèque Payot, 1976).

8   Miguel Abensour and Marcel Gauchet, introduction to *Le discours de la servitude volontaire*, xv.

9   Boétie, *Le discours de la servitude volontaire*, 41–56.

10   Pierre Leroux, "Discours sur la doctrine de l'humanité, deuxième partie. Notre principe d'organisation, Deuxième section. De la science politique jusqu'à nos jours, La Boétie, Hobbes, Montesquieu et Rousseau," *Revue sociale, ou solution pacifique du problème du proletariat*, August-September, 1847, 169–81. This text was partially reproduced in Pierre Leroux, *À la source perdue du socialisme français*, ed. Bruno Viard (Paris: Desclée de Brouwer, 1997), 395–96.

11   Leroux, "Discours sur la doctrine de l'humanité, deuxième partie," 172: "L'antithèse du *Contr'un* de La Boétie, c'est le livre de Thomas Hobbes, *Elemens philosophiques du citoyen, où les fondemens de la société civile sont découverts*. Hobbes avoit cinquante-huit ans quand il a publié ce livre à Paris en 1646. Il avait presque toujours vécu en France, il était versé dans notre littérature; comment n'aurait-il pas connu l'opuscule de La Boétie? Il n'aurait donc pas lu les essais de Montaigne? Cela est peu probable. On va voir que Hobbes, ce grand défenseur du *Un* déspotique et monarchique, doit avoir lu le *Contr'un*. Tout son dogmatisme n'est que le contrepied de la généreuse mais impuissante protestation du jeune *garçon de seize ans* parlant au nom du sentiment, et à l'honneur de la liberté contre les tyrans.". As is well-known, Hobbes lived in France around a dozen years, not "almost always."

12 Timothy J. Reiss and Hassan Melehy, "Utopia Versus State of Power, or Pretext of the Political Discourse of Modernity: Hobbes, Reader of La Boétie?" in *French Connections in the English Renaissance*, ed. Catherine Gimelli Martin and Hassan Melehy (London and New York: Routledge, 2016), 65–95, especially 65. In a similar perspective, see Wes Williams, "'Quel monstre de vice […] que la langue refuse de nommer?': Monsters and the Politics of Naming in *La Servitude volontaire* (and beyond)," *Early Modern French Studies* 44, no. 1 (2022): 86–101.

13 Cf. Jacques Viard, *Pierre Leroux et les socialistes européens* (Paris: Actes Sud, 1983); Idem, "Pierre Leroux ostracisé par la Sorbonne et réhabilité par l'église catholique," *Studi francesi* 16 (2012): 513–17; Carlo Ginzburg, preface to *Il vitello d'oro. Le radici della controversia antigiudaica*, by Pier Cesare Bori (Torino: Bollati Boringhieri, 2022), xii–xiii.

14 Charles Baudelaire, *Oeuvres complètes*, ed. Yves Gérard Le Dantec (Paris: Gallimard–Bibliothèque de la Pléiade, 1956), 694: "C'est dans tels phénomènes que la célèbre et orageuse formule de Pierre Leroux trouve sa veritable application." See also ibid, 972, in *L'art romantique*: "le paisible Pierre Leroux, dont les nombreux ouvrages sont comme un dictionnaire des croyances humaines, a écrit des pages sublimes et touchantes que l'auteur de *Jerôme Paturot* [Louis Reybaud] n'as peut-être pas lues."

15 Henri de Saint-Simon, *Opinions littéraires, philosophiques et industrielles* (Paris: Bossange Père, 1825), 5: "la révolution française qui a proclamé l'abolition de l'esclavage dans la nuit du 4 août, nuit décisive qui vit s'accomplir ce qu'avaient commencé Platon et Jésus Christ, et qui, arrachant le dernier fondement du vieil édifice social, permit de poser les bases d'un édifice tout nouveau. Cette grande et vraiment sublime détermination a rendu possible l'exécution de l'Évangile; elle a rendu les hommes égaux, et par conséquent capables, pour la première fois, de vivre en frères; elle a permis à la politique, qui ne pouvait être jusque là que l'art de tromper et d'opprimer, de devenir enfin une science, féconde, comme toutes les autres, en résultats salutaires."

16 Henri de Saint-Simon, *Nouveau Christianisme, dialogues entre un conservateur et un novateur* (Paris: Bossange Père, 1825), "avant-propos."

99

17   See Jacob L. Talmon, *Political Messianism. The Romantic Phase* (London: Praeger, 1960).

18   Leroux, "Discours sur la doctrine de l'humanité," 172: "puisé dans l'idéal, tire de la religion, incarné seulement jusqu'ici dans l'esprit de quelques-uns, jamais réalisé, est-il vrai en fait? …. conservera de la force tant que le problème d'une organisation sociale fondée sur l'égalité et sur la fraternité n'aura pas été résolu."

19   Pierre Leroux, *De l'égalité*, nouvelle éd. (Paris: Boussac, 1848), 65: "Supprimez l'égalité et Hobbes a raison. … Hobbes est le seul qui ait connu la vérité, et qui ait osé le dire. Mais l'égalité humaine n'était ni proclamée ni même comprise en aucune façon lorsque Hobbes écrivait."

20   Thomas Hobbes, *Elemens philosophiques du bon citoyen. Traicté politique où les fondemens de la société civile sont découverts, par Thomas Hobbes et traduicts en françois par un de ses amis* (Paris: V T. Pepingué et E. Maucroy, 1651).

21   Thomas Hobbes, *Le Corps politique*, trans. Samuel de Sorbière (1652), ed. Louis Roux (Saint-Etienne: Publications de l'Université de Saint-Etienne, 1977), 88.

22   Thomas Hobbes, *The Elements of Law Natural and Politic*, part II, *De corpore politico*, ed. J. C. A. Gaskin (Oxford: The University Press, 1928), ch. XXII, 128.

23   See footnote 5 in this chapter.

24   Hobbes, *The Elements of Law*, ch. XIX, 106–107. See also *Le Corps politique*, 52–53.

25   Hobbes, *The Elements of Law*, ch. XXI, 125. See also *Le Corps politique*, 84: "se soûmettre volontairement à la puissance d'un autre, comme l'on fait dans toute Republique." A reference to "voluntary offer of subjection" surfaces again in *The Elements of Law*, ch. XXII, 126.

26   Thomas Hobbes, *De Cive. The Latin Version*, ed. Howard Warrender (Oxford: Clarendon Press, 1983), 134.

27   Hobbes, *De Cive*, 134.

28   La Boétie, *Le discours*, 105.

29   La Boétie, *Le discours*, 108.

30   Hobbes, *The Elements of Law*, ch. XIX, 107.

31 La Boétie, *Le discours*, 115: "Celui qui vous maistrise tant n'a que deux yeulx, n'a que deux mains, n'a qu'un corps, et n'a autre chose que ce qu'a le moindre homme du grand et infini nombre de vos villes, sinon que l'avantage que vous luy faites pou vous destruire. D'ou a il pris tant d'yeulx dont il vous espie, si vous ne luy baillés? Comment a il tant des mains pour vous fraper, s'il ne les prend de vous? Les pieds don't il foule vos cités, d'ou les a s'ils ne sont de vostres? Comment a il aucun pouvoir sur vous, que par vous?" Here, as Delaruelle has pointed out ("L'inspiration antique," 43), La Boétie echoed a passage of Aristotle's *Politics,* reworked by Erasmus. See N. O. Keohane's perceptive comment in "The radical humanism of Étienne De La Boétie," *Journal of the History of Ideas* 38, no. 1 (1977):119–130, especially 129: "Long before Hobbes, La Boétie pointed out how the power of Leviathan is composed of the hands and eyes and labors of all those who make up the state."

32 La Boétie, *Le discours*, 116–117: "et de tant d'indignités que les bestes mesmes ou ne les sentiroient point, ou ne l'endureroient point, vous pouvés vous en delivrer si vous l'essaiés, non pas de vous en delivrer, mais seulement de le vouloir faire. Soiés resolus de ne servir plus, et vous voila libres; je ne veux pas que vous le poussies ou l'esbranlies; mais seulement ne le soustenés plus, et vous les verrés comme un grand colosse a qui on a desrobé la base, de son pois mesme fondre en bas et se rompre." On the texts reworked in this passage (Plutarch, Erasmus, Baldassar Castiglione), see Barrére, *L'humanisme et la politique*, 97.

33 See Quentin Skinner, *Hobbes and Republican Liberty* (Cambridge: Cambridge University Press, 2008), 185 ff. La Boétie is not mentioned in Horst Bredekamp, *Leviathan: Body Politic as Visual Strategy in the Work of Thomas Hobbes*, trans. and ed. Elizabeth Clegg (Berlin: De Gruyter, 2020).

34 See Saul Newman, "La Boétie and Republican Liberty: Voluntary Servitude and Non-Domination," *European Journal of Political Theory* 21, no. 1 (2022): 134–54, especially 145: "While the image here of the collective body of the tyrant might seem Hobbesian, it is also deeply ambiguous in the way it disturbs, rather than affirms, the foundations of political authority."

35   Claude Lefort, "Le nom d'Un," in La Boétie, *Le discours*, 267: "Au corps visible du tyran, qui n'en est qu'un parmi d'autres, s'attache l'image d'un corps sans égal, sans réplique, à la fois entièrement séparé de ceux qui le voient, en ceci entièrement rapporté à lui-même, et qui, tout voyant, tout agissant, ne laisserait rien subsister hors de soi. Image du pouvoir détaché, surplombant la masse des sans-pouvoir, maître de l'existence de tous et de chacun; mai aussi image de la société toute rassemblée et possèdant une seule et même identité organique."

36   See, for instance, the "anarcho-republican" interpretation of *La servitude volontaire* advanced by Newman in "La Boétie and Republican Liberty."

37   Stefano de la Boëtie [sic], *Il contr'uno: o della servitù volontaria*, trans. Pietro Fanfani, ed. Pietro Pancrazi (Florence: Le Monnier, 1944). Pancrazi dedicated the book "Alla memoria di Leone Ginzburg, morto per la libertà nella carceri di Regina Coeli in Roma, il 5 febbraio 1944."

Chapter Two

1   Carlo Ginzburg, "Clues" in *Clues, Myths, and the Historical Method*, trans. John and Anne Tedeschi (Baltimore: Johns Hopkins University Press, 1989), 97.

2   On Goodman's distinction between "autographic" and "allographic" arts, see Carlo Ginzburg, "Invisible Texts, Visible Images," in *Coping with the Past. Creative Perspectives on Conservation and Restoration*, ed. Pasquale Gagliardi, Bruno Latour, and Pedro Memelsdorff (Florence: Leo S. Olschki, 2010), 133–44, 157–60. On René Wellek's distinction, see Idem, "Text and Voice, Text vs Voice," in *L'Inquisizione romana, i giudici e gli eretici. Studi in onore di John Tedeschi*, ed. Andrea del Col and Anne Jacobson Schutte (Rome: Viella, 2017), 57, note 57.

3   Walter Benjamin, "On the Mimetic Faculty," in *Selected Writings*, vol. 2 (1927–1934), ed. Michael W. Jennings, Howard Eiland, and Gary Smith (Cambridge, MA: Belknap Press, 1999), 720–22.

4   Pascal David, "Bild," in *Vocabulaire* éuropéen *des philosophies. Dictionnaire des intraduisibles*, ed. Barbara Cassin (Paris: Seuil, 2004), 191–95.

5   Benjamin, "On the Mimetic Faculty," 721.

6   Walter Benjamin, "Das Kunstwerk im Zeitalter technischen Reproduzierbarkeit (Erste Fassung)," in *Gesammelte Schriften*, vol. 1, bk. 2, ed. Rolf Tiedemann and Hermann Schweppenhäuser (Frankfurt am Main: Suhrkump, 1991), 430–69, quote on 436.

7   On this issue see, in a perspective very different from the one suggested here, Sigrid Weigel, "Der Blitz der Erkenntnis—Malerei und Photographie als Palimpsest von Benjamins Bilddenken," in *Grammatologie der Bilder* (Berlin: Suhrkamp, 2015), 402–42.

8   Walter Benjamin, *The Arcades Project*, trans. Howard Eiland and Kevin McLaughlin (Cambridge, MA: The Belknap Press, 2003), 7.

9   Gustave Planche, "L'art et l'industrie (*De l'union des arts et de l'industrie*, par M. Léon de Laborde)" *Revue des deux mondes* 10 (1857): 185–210.

10   Léon de Laborde, *De l'union des arts et de l'industrie*, 2 vols. (Paris: Imprimerie Impériale, 1856); Idem, *Quelques idées sur la direction des arts et sur le maintien du goût public* (Paris: Imprimerie Impériale, 1856). The importance of this work has been duly emphasized by Pierre Francastel, *Art et technique au XIXe et XXe siècles* (Paris: Gallimard, 1956); Karlheinz Barck, "Kunst und Industrie bei Léon de Laborde und Gottfried Semper. Differente Aspekte der Reflexion eines epochengeschichtlichen Funktionwandels der Kunst," in *Art social und Art industriel. Funktionen der Kunst im Zeitalter des Industrialismus*, ed. Helmut Pfeiffer, Hans Robert Jauss, and Françoise Gaillard (Munich: W. Fink, 1987), 241–68.

11   Léon de Laborde, *Plan de la ville de Petra et de ses environs levé sur les lieux par Léon de Laborde* (1829); Léon de Laborde and Linant de Bellefonds, *Voyage de l'Arabie Pétrée* (Paris: Giard, 1830); Léon de Laborde and L.-M.-A. Linant de Bellefonds, *Pétra retrouvée: voyage de l'Arabie Pétrée* [1828], with preface and notes by Christian Augé and Pascale Linant de Bellefonds (Paris: Pygmalion, 1994).

103

12 Léon de Laborde, *Essais de gravure pour servir à une histoire de la gravure en bois* (Paris: J. Didot lAîné, 1833); Idem, *Histoire de la découverte de l'impression et de son application à la gravure, aux caractères mobiles et à la lithographie* (Paris: A. Éverat, ca. 1839); Idem, *Histoire de la gravure en manière noire* (Paris: J. Didot l'Aîné, 1839); Idem, *Débuts de l'imprimerie à Mayence et à Bamberg, ou Description des lettres d'indulgence du pape Nicolas V, "Pro regno Cypri," imprimées en 1454* (Paris: Techener; Strasbourg: Levrault; Leipzig: R. Weigell, 1840); Idem, *Débuts de l'imprimerie à Strasbourg ou Recherches sur les travaux mystérieux de Gutenberg dans cette ville et sur le procès qui lui fut intenté en 1439 à cette occasion* (Paris: Techener, 1840); Idem, *Notice des émaux, bijoux et objets divers exposés dans les galeries du Musée du Louvre* (Paris: Vinchon, 1853). See also *Catalogue des livres composant la bibliothèque de feu M. L.J.S.E. Marquis de Laborde ... ancien conservateur du Musée du Louvre ...* Paris 1871: an invaluable research tool.

13 Laborde, *De l'union*, I, 2.

14 "L'intelligence des choses de goût n'est plus un arcane, un saint des saints, où se tiennent barricadés les grands prêtres d'impénétrables mystères. La religion, les lettres, les sciences, les arts ont bien été successivement escamotées par quelques gens adroits qui ont maintenu le peuple dans l'ignorance, sous prétexte qu'il était incapable de profiter de l'initiation et trop disposé à en faire un mauvais usage; mais le progrès de l'humanité, avec l'assistance de Dieu, ont eu raison de ces entraves. Le christianisme a vulgarisé le culte de Dieu, l'imprimerie a vulgarisé les lettres, les vrais savants ont vulgarisé la science; l'industrie, c'est-à-dire le génie des arts appliqué, s'apprête à populariser les arts.

En est-on moins sincèrement religieux, pour l'être en communauté avec son prochain; moins profondément lettré parce qu'on ait son Cicéron et son Virgile imprimés, en même temps que cent mille autres lecteurs, au lieu de le posséder manuscrit avcec dix ou douze collègues; moins profondément savant, pour l'être plus pratiquement? Les arts, enfin, perdront-ils quelque chose de leur élévation pour avoir abaissé leurs regards sur la foule, auront-ils amoindri leur sommet en étendant leur base? Certes non." Laborde, *De l'union*, II, 26–27.

15   "Le Daguerréotype… a beaucoup fait parler, beaucoup fait écrire; je voudrais dire aussi mon mot à ce sujet. Je ne sais rien de si méprisable que tout ce qui tend à 'vulgariser l'art', comme on dit, et qui n'arrivera jamais qu'à faire de l'art vulgaire. L'homme de talent ou de genie s'élève jusqu'à l'art; l'art ne doit jamais s'abaisser complaisemment jusqu'à l'imbécile et au crétin." Alphonse Karr, *Les guêpes* (Paris: Figaro, 1839), 55. I am deeply grateful to Manfred Posani Loewenstein for having brought this passage to my attention.

16   "À peine la gravure, procédé reproducteur, admirablement employé par Albert Dürer, a-t-elle paru dans son aspect expressif, facile et populaire, que Raphael s'attache Marc-Antoine et forme cet élève à la plus parfaite compréhension de sa pensée, à la plus habile manière de rendre son dessin." Laborde, *De l'union,* I, 81.

17   "Aux premiers pas de toutes les grandes découvertes, nous avons vu hausser les épaules, hocher les têtes. Hier, c'était la vapeur et les chemins de fer; aujourd'hui, c'est l'electricité; demain, ce sera la locomotion aérienne; et ainsi chaque jour voit s'élever une idéc en face d'une masse d' objections. L'idée perce les nuages et les brouillards; elle resplendit sur l'humanité entière; et les myopes de dire aux incrédules: Il faut avouer qu'il fait jour. Il en sera de même de la vulgarisation de l'art." Laborde, *De l'union,* I, 39.

18   "L'intervention des machines a été, dans cette propagande de l'art, une époque et l'équivalent d'une révolution; les moyens reproducteurs sont l'auxiliaire démocratique par excellence. Contester cette action est aveugle; dédaigner cette influence serait d'un insensé; ne pas prévoir l'avenir de cette association du génie des arts avec la puissance des nouveaux moyens de production à bon marché, c'est d'un esprit borné. La fonte du bronze, qui multiplia les chefs-d'oeuvre de Phidias et des grands sculpteurs de l'antiquité, avait été accueillie par la Grèce avec reconnaissance; le moyen âge reçut comme un don du Ciel l'imprimerie, qui est l'écriture mécanique; hier la vapeur, cette éloquente expression de la société moderne, donnait ces bras puissants en aide à tous les produits de l'industrie imprégnés de l'influence des arts; aujourd'hui la photographie, ou l'art mécanique dans une perfection idéale, initie le monde aux beautés des creations divines et hu-

maines. Tous ces moyens réunis répandent jusque dans la cabane du paysan la copie habilement reproduite de l'objet d'art unique et de l'étoffe brodée à la main que le riche avait seul possédés." Laborde, *De l'union*, II, 75. This passage is quoted by Barck in "Kunst und Industrie," 250.

19 "C'est dans les premières années du XIXe siècle que, pour la première fois depuis l'antiquité, et à l'imitation des Romains de la décadence, qui firent des contrefaçons du vieux style grec et égyptien, on eut l'étrange idée de refaire du gothique. L'Angleterre, la première, s'éprit de cette fantaisie. Bien qu'elle n'eût pas cessé, surtout en province, de construire en style gothique, on peut dire que le mouvement produit à cette époque eut le caractère d'une réaction. Horace Walpole l'active, par manière de passe-temps, gaiement, et sans y mettre d'importance. Les ouvrages sérieux sur les antiquités gothiques composés par des Anglais, dans notre Normandie et chez eux, prouvent que dès lors la grande et belle architecture dérivée de l'antiquité ne satisfaisait plus les goûts de la nation, qu'il lui fallait une diversion, une distraction: on lui servit le gothique comme un hochet national." Laborde, *De l'union*, II, 359–60.

20 *Historical and descriptive essays accompanying a series of engraved specimens of the architectural antiquities of Normandy, edited by John Britton, the subjects measured and drawn by Augustus Pugin, and engraved by John and Henry Le Keux*, (London, printed for the proprietors, 1828).

21 Kenneth Clark, *The Gothic Revival. An Essay in the History of Taste* [1928], new ed. (Harmondsworth: Penguin, 1964), 66, referring to Augustus Pugin and Edward James Willson, *Specimens of Gothic architecture selected from various ancient edifices in England*, 2 vols (London: M. A. Nattali, 1821).

22 "Inutile de raconter longuement le retour et la vogue du gothique neuf. Il a fait son temps comme mode (...) Pas un café qui voulût aujourd'hui d'une décoration à ogives, pas un fabricant de meubles qui osât faire une chaise à croisillons et à lancettes; j'ai vu refuser à Paris, par le jury de l'Exposition de Londres, la dernière pendule en cathédrale gothique; seul j'ai voté pour son admission, comme ces vieux pêcheurs qui puisent de l'indulgence dans le souvenir de leurs fautes.

Mon erreur, cependant, n'avait pas été absolue, parce que mes études et mes voyages m'avaient préservé de l'engouement aveugle. De mes premiers pas, j'avais fait au gothique sa part, et elle me paraissait juste, bien qu'aujourd'hui je suis disposé même à en rabattre quelque chose. Peu importe. La part du gothique me semblait dès lors purement archéologique." Laborde, *De l'union*, II, 360–361.

23 "Je m'arrêtai en conséquence à cette conclusion: on étudiera dans les classes de l'Ecole des beaux-arts le byzantin, le roman et le gothique, dans la mésure qui sera nécessaire pour apprendre à restaurer les monuments construits dans ces styles, ainsi que pour leur accorder la place qui leur appartient dans l'histoire de l'art; mais on ne fera à aucun prix des pastiches de byzantin, de roman et de gothique.
Nous reprochera-t-on d'oublier que le style gothique est l'architecture chrétienne? Ceux qui répètent cette niaiserie veulent-ils exclure du christianisme tout ce qui a prié sous des nefs à plein cintre?" Laborde, *De l'union*, II, 361.

24 "Une figure purement païenne en marbre blanc, comme celle de Notre-Dame, à Bruges, et que l'on attribue à Michel-Ange, ne produira jamais rien, quelle que soit sa beauté comme oeuvre d'art. Il n y a là rien qui charme ou attire – c'est une déesse plus ou moins imposante, voilà tout." In the introduction to *Les vrais principes de l'architecture ogivale ou chrétienne: avec des remarques sur leur renaissance au temps actuel / remanié et dévoloppé d'après le texte anglais de A. W. Pugin par T. H. King* (Brussels et Leipzig: Mayer et Flatau, 1850), xxvii.

25 "... les Français, bien mieux tous les Français, sacrifieront leur dernier écu au luxe voyant et aussi au luxe élégant. Sous l'influence de ces dispositions, la nation entière s'est éprise du goût des arts, de l'amour des monuments, de la passion pour les images, autant de symptômes d'une renaissance populaire à laquelle je voudrais voir l'Etat concourir de tous ces efforts. Je dis renaissance populaire, car il ne s'agit plus, comme au VIIIe siècle, sous Charlemagne, comme au XIIIe siècle, sous saint Louis, comme au XVIe, sous François Ier, comme au XVIIe, sous Louis XIV, de la renaissance des arts à la cour de France, mais d'une renaissance aussi belle, aussi forte et plus féconde, parce qu'en descendant dans la rue elle s'étend à tout le pays." Laborde, *De l'union*, II, 12.

107

26 "Non, dit-on, nous n'excluons aucun style de l'architecture chrétienne, mais nous demandons qu'on revienne en France à notre architecture nationale. Ah! C'est un autre theme. Où prend-on notre nationalité? Comme ancienneté, au XIIe siècle, ce n'est pas remonter bien haut; comme territoire, dans l'ancien domaine royal, c'est-à-dire dans cinq ou six départments autour de Paris, c'est bien modeste; et en effet, avant le XIIe siècle, il n'y a pas de gothique, et hors de ces limites c'est un autre gothique, et au delà encore, de l'autre côté de la Loire ou dans la moitié de la France, ce n'est plus du gothique." Laborde, *De l'union*, II, 362.

27 "Mais où sont (…) les éléments d'une resurrection pareille, inouïe jusqu'ici dans les fastes de l'art? Où en est la nécessité, dans les conditions de la société actuelle? Où est la main puissante qui peut soulever une nation entière, au point de la faure rétrograder de quatre siècles en arrière? Où est l'exemple de tout un peuple qui ait rompu avec son présent et avec son avenir pour revenir à son passé?" Quoted in Eugène-Emmanuel Viollet-Leduc, *Du style gothique au dix-neuvième siècle* (Paris: V. Didron, 1846), 10.

28 "Ce qui soulève et soulévera une nation entière, messieurs, c'est votre long dédain pour nos monumens que vous louez aujourd'hui du bout de lèvres, et comme pour faire la part de l'opinion; c'est votre mépris superbe pour ces édifices vraiment nationaux, que ni l'engouement de la Renaissance pour l'antique, ni l'orgueil de Louis XIV qui repoussait tout ce qu'il n'avait pas élevé, ni l'indifférence du siècle dernier, n'ait pu anéantir ou sur notre sol, ou dans les souvenirs du people." Viollet-Leduc, *Du style gothique*, 27.

29 Laborde, *De l'union*, II, 75.

30 "La société change de face, elle ouvre un avenir indéfini d'association démocratique et de centralisation populaire qui met les intérêts de la communauté et la jouissance des plaisirs à la portée de tous. En politique, les assemblées déliberantes et leur vaste auditoire; en industrie, les concours de tout genre et les expositions universelles; pour la science, les grands amphithéatres des cours publiques ouverts aux ouvriers, les salles immenses des musées et des bibliothèques; pour l'armée, des éspaces couverts où l'on fait manoeuvrer des regiments en-

tiers d'infanterie et de cavalerie; pour la société, les grands clubs, les grands cafés; pour les plaisirs, les théatres de jour, les cirques, les hippodromes; pour les besoins des villes, les gares de chemins de fer, les halles et marches, les rues elles-mêmes couvertes et vitrées: tant le bien-être devient exigeant!" Laborde, *De l'union*, II, 476.

31   Benjamin, *The Arcades Project*, 915; for the German text, see Walter Benjamin, *Das Passagen-Werk*, in *Gesammelte Schriften*, vol. 5, bk. 2, ed. Rolf Tiedemann and Hermann Schweppenhäuser (Frankfurt am Main: Suhrkamp, 1982), 1222. A recent study on this topic, Jack Post, "The Telescoping of the Past through the Present. Antoine Wiertz and Walter Benjamin's Philosophy of (Art) History," *Image [and] Narrative* 15, no. 4 (2014): 40–58, is disappointing.

32   "Il nous est né, depuis peu d'années, une machine, l'honneur de notre époque, qui, chaque jour, étonne notre pensée et effraie nos yeux.
Cette machine, avant un siècle, sera le pinceau, la palette, les couleurs, l'adresse, l'habitude, la patience, le coup d'oeil, la touche, la pâte, le glacis, la ficelle, le modèle, le fini, le rendu.
Avant un siècle, il n'y aura plus de maçons en peinture: il n'y aura plus que des architectes, des peintres, dans toute l'acception du mot.
Qu'on ne pense pas que le daguerréotype tue l'art. Non, il tue l'oeuvre de la patience, il rend hommage à l'oeuvre de la pensée.
Quand le daguerréotype, cet enfant géant, aura atteint l'âge de maturité, quand toute sa force, toute sa puissance se seront developpées, alors le genie de l'art lui mettra tout à coup la main sur le collet et s'écriera: 'A moi! Tu es à moi maintenant! Nous allons travailler ensemble.'" Benjamin, *The Arcades Project*, 670; Benjamin, *Passagen-Werk*, 824; Antoine J. Wiertz, "La photographie," in *Oeuvres littéraires* (Paris: Libraire Internationale, 1870), 309.

33   [Maurice Joly] *Dialogue aux Enfers entre Machiavel et Montesquieu, ou la politique de Machiavel au XIXe siècle, par un contemporain* (Brussels: A. Mertens et Fils, 1864). Benjamin's absence of remarks on the source of the *Protocols* is pointed out by Jeffrey Mehlman: "Thoughts on the French Connection," in *The Paranoid Apocalypse, A Hundred-Year Retrospective on* The Protocols of the Elders of Zion, ed. Richard Landes and Steven T. Katz (New York: New York University Press,

2012), 95. See also Carlo Ginzburg, "Rappresentare il nemico. Sulla preistoria francese dei *Protocolli*," in *Il filo e le tracce. Vero falso finto* (Milano: Feltrinelli, 2006), 185–204.

34 "Il y a dix ans, chaque graveur sur bois inscrivait son nom en toutes lettres au bas d'une oeuvre sans importance; aujourd'hui, feuilletez les journaux et *Les Livres illustrés, Le Magasin pittoresques, L'illustration, Les Musées des Familles,* et autres publications pittoresques à bon marché, vous ne trouverez plus un nom au bas des gravures remarquables de toutes ces publications. La gravure en bois est toujours un art; mais chacun sent qu'une interpretation, même parfait, un fac-simile, même exact, de l'oeuvre d'autrui, n'est pas plus méritoire que de bien copier une lettre; et l'expéditionnaire du ministère ne met pas son nom au bas de sa copie." Laborde, *De l'union*, II, 78. On the basis of this and other passages, Karlheinz Barck, in his essay "Kunst und Industrie," which displays a quote from Walter Benjamin as a motto, interpreted Laborde's work, unconvincingly, as a conservative defense of *l'art pour l'art*.

35 Wiertz, "La photographie," *Oeuvres littéraires*, 310.

36 "Chose admirable! L'astre qu'avait éclairé en secret les chefs-d'oeuvre du génie, les popularise aujourd'hui en les traversant de ses regards. La démocratie de la beauté nous vient du soleil!" Charles Blanc, "Les dessins de Raphaël," *Gazette des Beaux-Arts* 4 (1859), 193–209, especially 198–99.

37 "Il [Laborde] s'attache notamment à démontrer que l'art doit cesser d'être une jouissance purement aristocratique, qu'il doit, au contraire, se répandre et se vulgariser; mais qu'il a besoin, dans ce but, de s'associer à l'industrie [...] À notre avis, cette extrême diffusion, cette 'vulgarisation', aménerait un résultat inévitable, infaillible: l'absorption de l'art par l'industrie..." *Rapport sur l'ouvrage de M. le comte de Laborde, intitulé* De l'union des arts et de l'industrie, *adressé à LL. EE. les ministres d'état et de la maison de l'Empereur, de l'instuction publique et des cultes, de l'agriculture, du commerce et des travaux publics* (Paris: Didot Frères, Fils et Cie, 1858), 4–6. An aria from Halévy's opera *La juive* ("Rachel quand du Seigneur") is famously mentioned in À *la recherche du temps perdu*.

38 For example, on October 11, 2022, artist Damien Hirst set fire to one thousand of his works, retaining them as NFTs: https://www.npr.org/2022/10/12/1128292149/artist-damien-hirst-burned-1000-paintings-nft-non-fungible-tokens.

Chapter Three

1 I developed this point in my book *Fear, Reverence, Terror. Five Essays in Political Iconography* (Calcutta: Seagull Books, 2017).

2 Voltaire, "Il faut prendre un parti ou Le principe du action. Diatribe (1772)," in *Oeuvres complètes*, Moland edition, vol. 28 (Paris: Garnier Frères, 1879), 517–54.

3 See Carlo Ginzburg, *Threads and Traces: True False Fictive*, trans. Anne C. Tedeschi and John Tedeschi (Berkeley-Los Angeles: University of California Press, 2012), 11–112.

4 Voltaire, "Il faut prendre un parti," 534: "Non seulement nous passons notre vie à tuer et à dévorer ce que nous avons tué, mais tous les animaux s'égorgent les uns les autres; ils y sont portés par un attrait invincible. Depuis les plus petits insectes jusqu'au rhinocéros et à l'éléphant, la terre n'est qu'un vaste champ de guerres, d'embûches, de carnage, de destruction; il n'est point d'animal qui n'ait sa proie, et qui, pour la saisir, n'emploie l'équivalent de la ruse et de la rage avec laquelle l'exécrable araignée attire et dévore la mouche innocente. Un troupeau de moutons dévore en une heure plus d'insectes, en broutant l'herbe, qu'il n'y a d'hommes sur la terre."; "qu'y a t il pourtant de plus abominable que de se nourrir continuellement de cadavres?"// "dans cette horrible scène de meurtres toujours renouvelés, on voit évidemment un dessein formé de perpétuer toutes les espèces par les cadavres sanglants de leurs ennemis mutuels. Ces victimes n'expirent qu'après que la nature a soigneusement pourvu à en fournir de nouvelles. Tout renaît pour le meurtre."

5 Alice M. Laborde, *La bibliothèque du Marquis de Sade au château de La Coste (en 1776)* (Geneva: Slatkine, 1991), 45: "'Grand recueil nécessaire,' liste de 1769: 10 vols, dont 6 par Voltaire." Jean Deprun remarks that in *La nouvelle Justine* Sade echoes Voltaire's *Questions de*

Zapata nearly in their entirety. See "Quand Sade récrit Fréret, Voltaire et d'Holbach," *Obliques* 12–13 (1977), 264.

6   Sade, *La Philosophie dans le boudoir*, in *Oeuvres*, vol. 3,ed. Michel Delon (Paris: Gallimard, 1998), 143–53. For the English translation, see Marquis de Sade, *Justine, Philosophy in the Bedroom, and Other Writings*, trans. Richard Seaver and Austryn Wainhouse (New York: Grove Press, 1965), 296–339.

7   Sade, *Justine*, 330.

8   Sade, *Justine*, 331.

9   Cf. Isaiah Berlin, *The Hedgehog and the Fox. An Essay on Tolstoy's View of History* (London: Weidenfeld and Nicolson, 1967), 48–82.

10   Joseph de Maistre, "Les soirées de Saint-Pétersbourg ou Entretiens sur le gouvernement temporal de la providence," in *Oeuvres complètes*, vol. 5 ed. Emmanuel Vitte (Lyon: Librairie Générale Catholique et Classique, 1892), 22–25; I quote from the English translation, Joseph de Maistre, "The Saint Petersburg Dialogues," in *The Works of Joseph de Maistre*, ed. and trans. Jack Lively (New York: Schocken Books, 1965), 251–53. A reference to this passage is found in Stephen Holmes, *The Anatomy of Antiliberalism* (Cambridge, MA: Harvard University Press, 1993), 31–32. See also Joseph de Maistre, "Considérations sur la France," in *Oeuvres*, ed. Pierre Glaudes (Paris: Bouquins, 2007), 218: "Il n'y a que violence dans l'univers: mais nous sommes gâtés par la philosophie moderne, qui a dit que *tout est bien*, tandis que le mal a tout souillé, et que, dans un sens très vrai, *tout est mal*, puisque rien n'est à sa place."

11   Joseph de Maistre, "Les soirées de Saint-Pétersbourg ou Entretiens sur le gouvernement temporal de la providence," in *Oeuvres complètes*, vol. 4, ed. Emmanuel Vitte (Lyon: Librairie Générale Catholique et Classique, 1891), 205 ff., especially 210.

12   Two critics referred to the famous passage by de Maistre on the hangman (see below) only to deny its sadistic overtones: see Isaiah Berlin, "Joseph de Maistre and the Origins of Fascism," in *The Crooked Timber of Humanity: Chapters in the History of Ideas*, 2nd ed. (Princeton: Princeton University Press, 2013), 121: "This is not a mere sadistic meditation about crime and punishment…"; Holmes, *The Anatomy of Antiliberalism*, 30: "neither this passage nor those depicting the intoxicating

112

horrors of war should be misconstrued as an expression of de Maistre's personal sadism." In both cases there has been a reference to "sadism" and its related adjective "sadistic"—not to Sade as a writer. In a similar metaphorical mode, Lebrun has evoked the name of Sade in commenting on a passage written by de Maistre in 1771, when he was eighteen: "Therefore man, in his quality as a sensible being, must do everything that pleases himself, and abstain from anything that would make him suffer. Therefore he can and must commit a crime when the crime pleases him (..) and if he did otherwise he would be a fool"—a reflection which ended with the traditional argument for the need of supernatural punishment as an instrument of morality. Richard A. Lebrun, *Joseph de Maistre. An Intellectual Militant* (Kingston and Montreal: McGill-Queens University Press, 1988), 21. At the time de Maistre wrote the preceding passage Sade had not begun to publish.

13 Mario Praz, *La carne, la morte e il diavolo nella letteratura romantica* (Rome: Società editrice "La Cultura," 1930); English translation: Mario Praz, *The Romantic Agony* (London: Collins, 1966).

14 De Maistre's secular attitude is stressed by Holmes, *The Anatomy of Antiliberalism*, 22.

15 Maistre, "Les soirées de Saint-Pétersbourg," in *Oeuvres complètes*, vol 4, 32–34. I quote from *The Works of Joseph de Maistre*, 191–92.

16 Carlo Ginzburg, "Making It Strange: The Prehistory of a Literary Device," in *Wooden Eyes. Nine Reflections on Distance*, trans. Martin Ryle and Kate Soper (London–New York: Columbia University Press, 2002), 123, 181–87.

17 Maistre, "Les soirées de Saint-Pétersbourg," *Oeuvres complètes*, vol. 5, 249 ff.: "Mon chien m'accompagne à quelque spectacle public, une exécution, par exemple… s'il voit du sang, il pourra frémir, mais comme à la boucherie. Là s'arrêtent ses connaissances, et tous les efforts des instituteurs intelligens, employés sans relâche pendant les siècles des siècles, ne le porteront jamais au-délà; les idées de morale, de souveraineté, de crime, de justice, de force publique, etc., attachées à ce triste spectacle, sont nulles pour lui." I quote from *The Works of Joseph de Maistre*, 222–23.

18   The published text reads slightly different: see Joseph de Maistre, *Considérations sur la France*, ed. Jean-Louis Darcel (Geneva: Slatkine 1980).

19   Jean Boissel, Introduction to *Considérations sur la France*, 31–33, quoted by Lebrun, *Joseph de Maistre*, 136–37.

20   P. Klossowski, *Sade mon prochain* (Paris: Editions du Seuil, 1947), 55 ("Esquisse du système de Sade"): "Et cependant, si cet ouvrage contient déjà les éléments de la philosophie anarchisante des versions ultérieures, il se présente encore comme l'illustration du dogme fondamental du christianisme: celui de la *réversibilité des mérites du sacrifice de l'innocent en faveur du coupable*; dogme que Joseph de Maistre reprendra vingt ans plus tard dans les *Soirées des Saint-Pétersbourg*. Encore un peu de temps et Sade et Maistre se retrouveront comme réunis dans la sensibilité de leur fraternel lecteur: Baudelaire." Klossowski alludes to the conclusion of Joseph de Maistre, "Eclaircissement sur les sacrifices," in *Oeuvres complètes*, vol. 5, 360.

21   "De Maistre et Edar Poe m'ont appris à raisonner," in Charles Baudelaire, "Mon Coeur mis à nu," *Oeuvres complètes*, ed. Yves Gérard Le Dantec (Paris: Gallimard, Bibliothèque de la Pléiade, 1954), 1234.

22   Michel Foucault, *Surveiller et punir. Naissance de la prison* (Paris: Gallimard, 1975), 9–13. See also Foucault's introduction to Georges Bataille, *Oeuvres complètes*, vol. 1, *Premiers écrits 1922–1940* (Paris: Gallimard, 1970), 5: "Nous devons à Bataille une grande part du moment où nous sommes." In the invaluable list of borrowings from the Bibliothèque Nationale, established by Jean-Pierre Le Bouler and Joëlle Bellec Martini, "Emprunts de Georges Bataille à la Bibliothèque Nationale (1922–1950)," *Oeuvres complètes*, vol. 12 (Paris: Gallimard, 1988), 551–621, Maistre's name does not show up. But this negative evidence is inconclusive: the only work by Sade, whom Bataille started reading in 1926, is listed in 1939 (#761).

23   Jean-Denis Bredin, *L'Affaire* (Paris: Julliard, 1983), 11–15, prologue: "La parade de Judas."

24   Henri Hubert and Marcel Mauss, "Essai sur la nature et les fonctions du sacrifice," *L'Année Sociologique* 2 (1897–1898; issued in 1899): 28–138, especially 136–37: "c'est une fonction sociale parce que le sacri-

fice se rapporte à des choses sociales."; "On comprend dès lors ce que peut être la fonction du sacrifice, abstraction faite des symboles par lesquels le croyant s'exprime à lui même"; "Le dieu, qui est en même temps le sacrifiant, ne fait qu'un avec la victime et parfois même avec le sacrificateur. ... Voilà comment la conception d'un dieu se sacrifiant pour le monde a pu se produire et est devenue, même pour les peuples le plus civilisés, l'expression la plus haute et comme la limite idéale de l'abnégation sans partage."; "Or, ce caractère de pénétration intime et de séparation, d'immanence et de transcendance est, au plus haut degré, distinctif des choses sociales. Elles aussi existent à la fois, selon le point de vue auquel on se place, dans et hors l'individu. On comprend dès lors ce que peut être la fonction du sacrifice, abstraction faite des symboles par lesquels le croyant s'exprime à lui même. C'est une fonction sociale parce que le sacrifice se rapporte à des choses sociales."; "Ces expiations et ces purifications générales, ces communions, ces sacralisations de groupes, ces créations de génies de villes donnent ou renouvellent périodiquement à la collectivité, représentée par ses dieux, ce caractère bon, fort, grave, terrible, qui est un des traits essentiels de toute personnalité sociale." In May 1898 Mauss wrote to Henri Hubert from Oxford: "Ce travail sur le sacrifice m'aura gâté cet année." M. Fournier, *Marcel Mauss* (Paris: Fayard, 1994), 133–34.

25 Émile Durkheim, *Lettres à Marcel Mauss*, ed. Philippe Besnard and Marcel Fournier (Paris: Presses universitaires de France, 1998), 96: "Au moment où les trois hommes [Durkheim, Mauss and Hubert] s'attaquent à la question du sacrifice, c'est un débat autour du sacrifice sur l'autel de la raison d' État qui éclate au grand jour l'affaire Dreyfus."

26 Edward Evans-Pritchard, *A History of Anthropological Thought*, ed. André Singer (London: Basic Books, 1981), 176–77.

27 Steven Lukes, *Émile Durkheim* (London: Penguin Books, 1973), 339, quotes from Durkheim, "L'individualisme et les intellectuels," *Revue bleue*, 4th series, 10 (1898), 7–13: "Essentiellement, elle n'est autre chose qu'un ensemble de croyances et de pratiques collectives d'une particulière autorité." For the English translation, see Émile Durkheim, "Individualism and the Intellectuals," *Political Studies* 17 (1969): 14–30, especially 25.

28 Daniel Lindenberg, introduction to *De Jaurès à Léon Blum*, by Hubert Bourgin [1938], new ed. (Paris: Gordon and Breach, 1970), 218–219: "[D.] c'était une figure hyératique. Sa mission était religieuse... Constituer la sociologie, déterminer les lois de l'existence et du développement de la société, c'était, pour lui, poser et asseoir les fondements d'une morale certaine, contraignante, impérative, comme peuvent l'être les lois de la physique pour les applications de cette science. C'était aussi fournir à l'homme moderne de quoi satisfaire à ses aspirations religieuses, la société bien policée devenant le souverain tout-puissant qui commande justement et qui mérite d'être aimé." The first sentence is quoted in Fournier, *Marcel Mauss*, 36.

29 [29] See Roger Caillois and Georges Bataille, "Le pouvoir," in *Le Collège de Sociologie (1937–1939)*, ed. Denis Hollier (Paris: Gallimard, 1995), 169–198; Pierre Klossowski, "Le marquis de Sade et la Révolution," in ibid, 502–532; Roger Caillois, "Sociologie du bourreau," in ibid, 543–568. Cf. Georges Bataille, *Lettres à Roger Caillois, 4 août 1935–4 février 1959*, ed. Jean-Pierre Le Bouler (Paris: Folle Avoine, 1987), plate 1: "Collège de Sociologie, année 1937–1938. Liste des exposés": Samedi 20 novembre 1937: "La sociologie sacrée et les rapports entre 'société,' 'organisme,' 'être'" par Georges Bataille et Roger Caillois; Samedi 2 avril 1938: "La sociologie sacrée du monde contemporain," par Georges Bataille et Roger Caillois."

30 The unexpected role played by de Maistre in the debates at the Collège de Sociologie is pointed out by Daniel Lindenberg, *Les années souterraines (1937–1947)* (Paris: La Decouverte, 1990), 78.

31 Cf. Carlo Ginzburg, "Germanic Mythology and Nazism. Thoughts on an Old Book by Georges Dumézil," in Idem, *Clues, Myths, and the Historical Method*, 114–131, 197–201, and especially 129. Note: "Sacred theology" on 130 should be corrected to "sacred sociology." See also "Mitologia germanica e nazismo. Su un vecchio libro di Georges Dumézil," in Idem, *Miti emblemi spie. Morfologia e storia* (Torino: Einaudi, 1986), 231.

32 Svend Ranulf, "Scholarly Forerunners of Fascism," *Ethics* 50 (1939): 16–34; Berlin, "Joseph de Maistre and the Origins of Fascism."

116

33 *Le Collège de Sociologie*, 194–195: "C'est en tout cas seulement depuis un petit nombre d'années que le crucifié a été menacé en Allemagne et en Italie par des images de puissance qui écartent toute idée de tragédie, toute idée de mise à mort du roi. Le faisceau italien tel qu'il figure sur le ventre de toutes les locomotives est d'ailleurs à cet égard plus chargé de signification precise que la croix gammée. Le faisceau du licteur était en effet à Rome l'insigne des magistrats à *imperium* tels que les consuls et les préteurs: il représentait essentiellement le pouvoir militaire qui appartenait à ces magistrats et qui se trouvait régulièrement lié au pouvoir, proprement religieux, de prendre les augures. Il faut surtout insister sur le fait que la hache du licteur n'était que l'instrument des éxécutions capitales. C'est ainsi l'instrument de la mise à mort des sujets qui est opposé ostensiblement à l'image du roi supplicié." For the English translation, see *The College of Sociology (1937–39)*, ed. Denis Hollier (Minneapolis: University of Minnesota Press, 1988), 125–36, especially 135. I quoted this passage in *Miti emblemi spie*, 230, as an example of Bataille's fascination with fascism. The same passage has been quoted, in a different perspective, by Cristiano Grottanelli, *Il sacrificio* (Roma-Bari: Laterza, 1999), 99.

34 Pierre Klossowski, "Le Marquis de Sade et la Révolution," February 7, 1939, in *Le Collège de Sociologie*, 529: "on imagine ici, comme sous-jacente à la Révolution, une sorte di conspiration morale … qui se fût servie de deux méthodes: une méthode exotérique pratiquée par Joseph de Maistre dans sa sociologie de péché originel, et une méthode ésotérique infiniment complexe *qui consiste à prendre le masque de l'athéisme pour combattre l'athéisme.*" See also *The College of Sociology*, 218–47, especially 230–31.

35 Roger Caillois, "Sociologie du bourreau," February 21, 1939, in *Le Collège de Sociologie*, 568: "il n'y a pas de société assez totalement conquise par les puissances de l'abstraction pour que les mythes et les réalités qui lui donnent naissance perdent en elle tout droit et tout pouvoir."; *The College of Sociology*, 247.

36 See Marina Galletti in her preface to Georges Bataille, *L'apprenti sorcier*, ed. Marina Galletti (Editions de la Différence, 1999), 12, who mentions, besides (and against) my essay "Germanic Mythology and

Nazism," Jacqueline Risset, "Le jour accusant de la pensée lente," *Lignes* 14 (1991): 73–92 and Bernard Sichère, "Bataille et les fascistes," *La règle du jeu* 8–9 (septembre 1992–janvier 1993). Further bibliography can be found in Marina Galletti, "Le monstre souterrain," in *Georges Bataille après tout*, ed. Denis Hollier (Paris: Belin, 1995), 267 ff. The ambiguity of the Collège towards fascism is stressed in Lindenberg, *Les années souterraines*, 57–97.

37 See Walter Benjamin, *Selected Writings, 1935–1938*, vol. 3, ed. Howard Eiland and Michael W. Jennings (Cambridge, MA: Belknap Press, 2002), 426.

38 Michel Vovelle's introduction to Friedrich Sieburg, *Robespierre* (Paris: Mémoire du Livre, 2003) is exceedingly reticent on Sieburg's political attitude (as well as on Klossowski's co-operation with him: see 20 n. 1). According to Vovelle (13), in 1935 Sieburg was not yet a Nazi. Yet in 1934 Thomas Mann had noted in his journal that Sieburg was a "well-known agent of the [German] Ministry of Propaganda": see Harro Zimmermann, *Friedrich Sieburg – Aesthet und Provokateur. Eine Biographie* (Göttingen: Wallstein Verlag, 2015), 185. Two more books (which I have not seen) by Sieburg were translated by Klossowski: *Sur un brise-glace soviétique: "le Malyguine"* (1932), and *Le Nouveau Portugal, portrait d'un vieux pays* (1938).

39 Friedrich Sieburg, *France d'hier et de demain*, preface by Bernard Grasset (Paris: Groupe "Collaboration," 1941). See Barbara Lambauer, *Otto Abetz et les Français ou l'envers de la collaboration*, preface by Jean-Pierre Azéma (Paris: Fayard, 2001), 242 and *passim*. For an apologetic portrait see Cecilia von Buddenbrock, *Friedrich Sieburg 1893–1964. Un journaliste allemand à l'épreuve du siècle*, preface by D. Venner (Paris: Éditions de Paris, 1999).

40 Bataille, *L'apprenti sorcier*, 111–12. "Sur le charactère archaïque et insoutenable des positions traditionnelles, je n'ai pas l'ombre d'un doute …. Je n'ai pas de doute quant au plan sur lequel nous devrions nous placer: cela ne peut être que celui du fascisme lui-même, c'est-à-dire le plan mythologique. Il s'agit donc de poser des valeurs participant d'un nihilisme vivant, à la mesure des impératifs fascistes." The letter is conjecturally dated February 14, 1934.

41   Bataille, *L'apprenti sorcier*, 263–64: "Les droites ont su mettre à profit l'expérience communiste et emprunter une partie des méthodes de leurs adversaires. Nous sommes assurés que le réciproque est aussi nécessaire." On Pierre Kaan, see Galletti's introduction (12 ff.), and the anthology "Visages de la Résistance," *La liberté de l'esprit* 16 (Lyon: La Manufacture, 1987).

42   Michel Surya, *Georges Bataille: La mort à l'oeuvre* (Paris: Gallimard, 1987), 239–40, suggests that André Masson might have played a role in Bataille's evolution. It should be noted that there was a "Sade group" in Contre-Attaque: see Bataille, *Lettres à Roger Caillois*, 59 n. 2.

43   Cf. Pierre-Antoine Fabre, "Les jésuites au Collège," in "Georges Bataille d'un monde à l'autre," *Critique* 788–789 (2013), 59–69.

44   Bataille, *L'apprenti sorcier*, 281–82: "communauté créatrice de valeurs", "la fonction de destruction et de décomposition mais comme achèvement et non comme négation de l'être", "ascèse positive... discipline individuelle positive"; "l'accomplissement universel de l'être personnel dans l'ironie du monde des animaux"; "prendre sur soi la perversion et le crime non comme valeurs exclusives mais comme devant être integrés dans la totalité humaine"; "Affirmer la valeur de la violence et de la volonté d'agression en tant qu'elles sont la base de la toute-puissance."

45   Bataille, *L'apprenti sorcier*, 279–81.

46   See Pierre Andler [Pierre Dugan], "Notes sur le fascisme," *L'apprenti sorcier*, 295–97, dated April 17, 1936.

47   Surya, *Georges Bataille*, 250–51, in rejecting the "insinuations" that Bataille would have been fascinated by fascism, admits that Pierre Dugan's text on "surfascisme" is questionable ("douteux"). Dugan's "Notes sur le fascisme," however, is simply an awkward paraphrase of Bataille's text written two weeks before.

48   Georges Bataille, "Propositions," *Acéphale*, January 21, 1937, 17.

49   Raymond Queneau, "Le mythe et l'imposture" (February 1939), in *Le voyage en Grèce* (Paris: Gallimard, 1973), 151–55.

50   Raymond Queneau, *Traité des vertus démocratiques*, ed. Emmanuël Souchier (Paris: Gallimard, 1993), 41–42. The publication of Maistre's project (*La Franc-Maçonnerie. Mémoire inédit au duc de Brunswick*

119

[1782], ed. Rieder [Paris, 1925]) had been announced by René Gué-non, *Etudes sur la Franc-Maçonnerie et le compagnonnage* (Paris: Edi-tions traditionnelles, 1964), 19–30: "Un projet de Joseph de Maistre pour l'union des peuples" (1927). In 1936–37 Queneau read Maistre's *Les Soirées de Saint-Pétersbourg* and *Du pape*.

51 See Roger Caillois, "Confréries, orders, sociétés secretes, églises," in *Le Collège de Sociologie*, 169–98; Hans Mayer, "Les rites des associa-tions politiques dans l'Allemagne romantique," in *Le Collège de Soci-ologie*, 217–244; 607–640. There is no written record of the talk de-livered by Bataille on January 24, 1939, on "Hitler and the Teutonic Order," mentioned on 215–17.

52 Bataille, *L'apprenti sorcier*, 367–78, especially 372–73: "une tentative de passer de la connaissance à l'acte"; "Or ce tissu nouveau est pré-cisément de la même nature que celui des sociétés primitives; il est mythique et rituel, il se forme avec vigueur autour d'images chargées des valeurs affectives les plus fortes; il se forme dans les vastes mouve-ments de foule réglés par un cérémonial introduisant les symboles qui subjuguent.'"

53 Alphonse de Châteaubriant, *La gerbe des forces* (Paris: Grasset, 1937), partially republished in Idem, *Procès posthume d'un visionnaire* (Paris: Nouvelles Editions Latines, 1987), 49–173. Roger Caillois, "L'esprit des sectes," in *Instincts et société. Essais de sociologie contemporaine* (Par-is: Gonthier, 1964), 62–114, especially 66. This essay, originally pub-lished in Mexico (in Spanish), was republished in *Fisiología de Levia-tán* (Buenos Aires: Editorial Sudamericana, 1946), 17–76.

54 George Mosse, "On Homosexuality and French Intellectuals," in Idem, *The Fascist Revolution: Towards a general Theory of Fascism* (New York: Howard Fertig, 1999), 175–92.

55 "Kojève nous a écoutés, mais il a écarté notre idée. Àses yeux, nous nous mettions dans la position d'un prestidigidateur qui demande-rait à ses tours de prestidigitation de le faire croire à la magie." *Le Col-lège de Sociologie*, 67, quoting Roger Caillois, "Entretien avec Gilles Lapouge," *La Quinzaine littéraire* 70, June 16–30, 1970.

56 Bataille, "L'apprenti sorcier," in *Le Collège de Sociologie*, 302–326, espe-cially 325; Bataille, "The Sorcerer's Apprentice," in *The College of Soci-*

ology, 12–23, especially 23. Queneau's essay "Le mythe et l'imposture" is a critical reaction to this piece.

57 Patrick Waldberg, "Acéphalogramme" [1995], in Bataille, *L'apprenti sorcier*, 584–98. A more elusive version of the story appears in "Vers un nouveau mythe?" [letters by Patrick Waldberg to Isabelle Waldberg, by Robert Lebel to Patrick Waldberg, by Georges Duthuit to André Breton], *VVV* 4 (1944), 41–49; see also Patrick Waldberg and Isabelle Waldberg, *Un amour acéphale, Correspondance 1940–1949*, ed. Michel Waldberg (Paris: Editions de la Différence, 1992). Another version has been given by Caillois, *Instincts et société*, 65–67; Idem, *Approches de l'imaginaire* (Paris: Gallimard, 1974), 59, partially translated into English as Roger Caillois and Susan Lanser, "The *Collège de Sociologie*: The Paradox of an Active Sociology," *Substance* 4, nos. 11–12 (1975): 61–64. See also Marina Galletti, "Una comunità bicefala. Acéphale e il Collège de Sociologie," in Idem, *La comunità "impossibile" di Georges Bataille. Da "Masses" ai "Difensori del male"* (Torino: Edizioni Kaplan, 2008), 90–112.

58 Fournier, *Marcel Mauss*, 689–91; Marcel Mauss, *Ecrits politiques*, ed. Marcel Fournier (Paris: Fayard, 1997), 766–67, letters to Svend Ranulf, November 6, 1936, and May 8, 1939. See also Steven Lukes, *Émile Durkheim* (London: Allen Lane, 1973), 338–39, note 71: "Durkheim, and after him, the rest of us are, I believe, those who founded the theory of the authority of the collective *représentation*. One thing that, fundamentally, we never foresaw was how many large modern societies, that have more or less emerged from the Middle Ages in other respects, could be hypnotized like Australians are by their dances, and set in motion like a children's roundabout. This return to the primitive had not been the object of our thoughts. We contented ourselves with several allusions to crowd situations, while it was a question of something quite different. We also contented ourselves with proving that it was in the collective mind [*dans l'esprit collectif*] that the individual could find the basis and sustenance for his liberty, his independence, his personality and his criticism [*critique*]. Basically, we never allowed for the extraordinary new possibilities… I believe that all this is a real tragedy for us, too powerful a verification of things that we had indicated and

the proof that we should have expected this verification through evil rather than a verification through goodness [*le bien*]."

59   See *The College of Sociology*, 347–50.

60   George L. Mosse, "Caesarism, Circuses and Monuments," *The Journal of Contemporary History* 6, no. 2 (1971): 167–182, reprinted in *Masses and Man: Nationalist and Fascist Perceptions of Reality* (New York: Howard Fertog, 1980), 104–18; Idem, *The Nationalization of the Masses. Political Symbolism and Mass Movements in Germany from the Napoleonic Wars through the Third Reich* (New York: Howard Fertig, 1975).

Chapter Four

1   Robert K. Merton, "The Self-fulfilling Prophecy," *The Antioch Review* 8, no. 2 (1948): 193–210, especially 195; also in Robert K. Merton, *Social Theory and Social Structure*, enl. ed. (New York: The Free Press, 1968), 475–490. There is an allusion to "self-fulfilling prophecy" in Robert E. Bartholomew and Hilary Evans, *Panic Attacks: Media Manipulation and Mass Delusion* (Stroud, Gloucestershire: The History Press, 2004), 114.

2   Merton, "The Self-fulfilling Prophecy," 195.

3   Craig Calhoun, "Remembering Robert K. Merton," *Items and Issues* 4, nos. 2–3 (2003): 12–14.

4   See note 55 in Chapter 3.

5   Merton, "The Self-fulfilling Prophecy," 210.

6   Cf. Franco Venturi, *Jean Jaurès e altri storici della Rivoluzione francese* (Torino: Einaudi, 1948), 187–94, emphasizes the element of "moderno volterrianesimo" shared by the two books. See my essay "La posverdad: un viejo asunto nuevo," in *Verdad, historia y posverdad. La construcción de narrativas en las humanidades*, ed. Miguel Giusti (Lima: Fondo Editorial PUCP, 2020), 13–38.

7   Marc Bloch, "Réflexions d'un historien sur les fausses nouvelles de la guerre," *Revue de synthèse historique* 33 (1921), 13–35. Published in English as "Reflections of a Historian on the False News of the War," trans. James P. Holoka, *Michigan War Studies Review*, July 2013. Cf. Marc Bloch and Joseph Bédier, *Storia psicologica della prima Guerra*

mondiale, ed. Francesco Mores (Rome: Castelvecchi, 2015). Two further essays by the present writer may be added to these bibliographical references: "A proposito della raccolta dei saggi storici di Marc Bloch," in *Studi medievali* 3, no. 6 (1965), 335–353; introduction to Marcel Bloch, *I re taumaturghi. Studi sul carattere sovrannaturale attribuito alla potenza dei re particolarmente in Francia e in Inghilterra* (Torino: Einaudi, 1973), xi–xix. See also Filippo de Vivo, "Microhistories of Long-Distance Information: Space, Movement and Agency in the Early Modern News," Supplement 14, *Past and Present* 242 (2019): 179–214, especially 213–14.

8   Venturi, *Jean Jaurès*, 188.

9   Robert K. Merton, "The Thomas Theorem and the Matthew Effect," *Social Forces* 74, no. 2 (1995): 379–424.

10   See Robert A. Nye, *The Origins of Crowd Psychology. Gustave le Bon and the Crisis of Mass Democracy in the Third Republic* (London: Sage Publications, 1975); Yvon J. Thiec, "Gustave Le Bon, prophète de l'irrationalisme de masse," in *Revue française de sociologie* 22, no. 3 (1981): 409–28; Benoit Marpeau, *Gustave Le Bon. Parcours d'un intellectuel (1841–1931)* (Paris: CNRS Editions, 2000). See also Elena Bovo, "Naissance d'une science controversée:la 'psychologie des foules,'" *La Clé des Langues*, March 6, 2017, http://cle.ens-lyon.fr/italien/civilisation/xvie-xixe/naissance-d-une-science-controversee-la-psychologie-des-foules-.

11   See Emilio Gentile, *Il capo e la folla, La genesi della democrazia recitativa* (Bari: Laterza, 2016), 149–156, especially 149: "Antirivoluzionario ma non reazionario."

12   Gustave Le Bon, *Rôle des Juifs dans la civilisation* (Paris: Amis de Gustave Le Bon, 1985), originally published in *Revue scientifique*, September 29, 1888, in response to F. Hément and the director of the *Revue*, Charles Richet.

13   See Olivier Bosc, "Gustave Le Bon, un mythe du XXe siècle?" *Mil neuf cent. Revue d'histoire intellectuelle* 28 (2010): 101–120.

14   Georges Lefebvre, "Foules révolutionnaires" (1932), in Idem, Études *sur la Révolution française*, with an introduction by Albert Soboul, 2nd ed. (Paris: Presses universitaires de France, 1963), 371–392, especially 371.

123

15   Michael Gamper, *Masse Lesen, Masse Schreiben. Eine Diskurs- und Imaginationsgeschichte der Menschenmenge 1765–1930* (Bonn: Fink, 2007), 29. Sigmund Freud (who used the word *Massen*) pointed out the difference between *masses* and *foules* in his discussion on Le Bon's *Psychologie des foules*. John Strachey translated Le Bon's *foules* and Freud's *Massen* as *groups*: an obviously untenable choice. See Sigmund Freud, *Group Psychology and the Analysis of the Ego*, trans. James Strachey, in *The Major Works* (Chicago: Enciclopaedia Britannic, 1980), 665–670.

16   Gustave Le Bon, *Psychologie des foules*, 2nd ed. (Paris: Félix Alcan, 1906), 12: "l'avènement des classes populaires à la vie politique, c'est-à-dire, en réalité, leur transformation progressive en classes dirigeantes. … Aujourd'hui les revendications des foules deviennent de plus en plus nettes, et ne vont pas à moins qu'à détruire de fond en comble la société actuelle, pour la ramener à ce communisme primitive qui fut l'état normal de tous les groupes humains avant l'aurore de la civilisation."; for the English translation, see Gustave Le Bon, *The Crowd: A Study of the Popular Mind* (London : T.F. Unwin, 1903), 15–16.

17   Le Bon, *Psychologie des foules*, 43.

18   Le Bon, *Psychologie des foules*, 11.

19   Robert Merton missed this point in his introduction to Gustave Le Bon, *The Crowd: A Study of the Popular Mind* (New York: Viking Press, 1960).

20   Le Bon, *Psychologie des foules*, 14: "La connaissance de la psychologie des foules constitue la resource de l'homme d'État qui veut, non pas les gouverner—la chose est devenue aujourd'hui bien difficile—mais tout au moins ne pas être trop complètement gouverné par elles."; Le Bon, *The Crowd*, 21.

21   Gentile, *Il capo e la folla*, 149–150.

22   Le Bon, *Psychologie des foules*, 25: "l'impulsivité, l'irritabilité, l'incapacité de raisonner, l'absence de jugement et d'esprit critique, l'exagération des sentiments, et d'autres encore, qu'on observe également chez les êtres appartenant à des formes inférieures d'évolution, telles que la femme, le sauvage et l'enfant."; Le Bon, *The Crowd*, 40.

23   Le Bon, *Psychologie des foules*, 21; Le Bon, *The Crow*d, 33.

24 Le Bon, *Psychologie des foules*, 29; Le Bon, *The Crowd*, 50.

25 Le Bon, *Psychologie des foules* (Paris: Félix Alcan, 1905), 9: "Les phéno-mènes sociaux visibles paraissent être la résultante d'un immense tra-vail inconscient, inaccessible le plus souvent à notre analyse."; Le Bon, *The Crowd*, 6.

26 Le Bon, *Psychologie des foules*, 35: "les foules son trop régies par l'in-conscient, et trop soumises par conséquent à l'influence d'hérédités séculaires, pour n'être pas extrêmement conservatrices."; Le Bon, *The Crowd*, 62.

27 Le Bon, *Psychologie des foules*, 115; Le Bon, *The Crowd*, 218.

28 Le Bon, *Psychologie des foules*, 116–117: "Le meneur doit avoir péné-tré, au moins d'une façon inconsciente, la psychologie des foules, et savoir comment leur parler. Il doit surtout connaître la fascinante in-fluence des mots, des formules et des images. Il doit posséder une élo-quence spéciale, composée d'affirmations énergiques—dégagées des preuves—et d'images impressionnantes, encadrées de raisonnements fort sommaires."; Le Bon, *The Crowd*, 221. See also *Psychologie des foules*, 105 ff. and *The Crowd*, 150: "Crowds always, and individuals as a rule, stand in need of ready-made opinions on all subjects. The popularity of these opinions is independent of the measure of truth or error they contain, and is solely regulated by their prestige." The im-portance of these remarks has been missed by Francesco Gallino, *In-conscio e politica in Gustave Le Bon* (Rome: Aracne, 2021), 117 ff.

29 Freud, *Group Psychology*, 669.

30 "Ho letto tutta l'opera di Gustavo Le Bon; e non so quante volte abbia riletto la sua *Psicologie delle folle*. E' un'opera capitale, alla quale an-cor oggi spesso ritorno," in Renzo De Felice, *Mussolini il rivoluziona-rio, 1883–1920*, intr. Dello Cantimori (Torino: Einaudi, 1965), 467, quoting Benito Mussolini, *Opera omnia*, ed. Edoardo and Duilio Su-smel, vol. 22 (Rome: La Fenice, 1957), 156. Mussolini's name is barely mentioned in Damiano Palano, *Il potere della moltitudine, L'invenzio-ne dell'inconscio collettivo nella teoria politica e nelle scienze sociali ita-liane tra Otto e Novecento* (Milan: Vita e Pensiero, 2002).

31 "Il suo [Mussolini's] sguardo attira con forza magnetica migliaia di occhi nella sfera della sua volontà, scruta quegli occhi, mentre cerca

125

di immedesimarsi nell'animo di questo o quell'individuo, i cui tratti per qualche ragione eccitano la sua attenzione. Ma il più delle volte è la magia reciproca di due grandezze che s'incrocia e incrociandosi sprizza faville. Una di queste grandezze è la Massa, che sente l'incanto dell'Uomo perché sa che è uno dei suoi, perché sa che è il suo signore," in "La personalità del Duce," in *Mussolini e il suo fascismo*, ed. Curt Gutkind, intr. Benito Mussolini (Florence: Merlin-Le Monnier, 1926), 3–4 (the text, unsigned, was certainly written by the editor). Gutkind was a tragic figure: a committed Fascist, at that time a *lettore* at the University of Florence, he later became professor at Heidelberg; in 1933, having been ejected as Jewish, he managed to teach in England for a short time; then was deported as an enemy alien to Canada; in July 1940 the ship on which he was travelling was hit by a German torpedo, and he died. See Patrizia Guarnieri's entry in *Intellettuali in fuga dal regime fascista. Migranti, esuli e rifugiati per motivi politici e razziali* http://intellettualinfuga.fupress.com/schede/indice/6.

32   Emil Ludwig, *Colloqui con Mussolini. Riproduzione delle bozze della prima edizione con le correzioni autografe del duce* (Milan: A. Mondadori, 1950), 64.

33   Benito Mussolini, "Preludio al Machiavelli," in *Scritti e Discorsi di Benito Mussolini. Il 1924* (Milan: Ulrica Hoepli, 1934), 1–10. See also Franco Biasutti, "Mussolini interprete di Machiavelli," in *Machiavelli, tempo e conflitto*, ed. Riccardo Caporali, Vittorio Morfino, and Stefano Visentin (Udine: Itinerari filosofici, 2014), 21–33. Here I am using a passage from my book *Nevertheless. Machiavelli, Pascal* (London: Verso: 2022), 108–110.

34   Mussolini, "Preludio al Machiavelli," 107–08: "Machiavelli è uno spregiatore degli uomini [...] Di tempo ne è passato, ma se mi fosse lecito giudicare i miei simili e contemporanei, io non potrei in alcun modo attenuare il giudizio di Machiavelli, Dovrei, forse, aggravarlo."

35   Emil Ludwig, *Talks with Mussolini,* translated by Eden and Cedar Paul (Boston: Little, Brown, and Company, 1933), 126–127.

36   Niccolò Machiavelli, *The Art of War*, ed. and trans. Peter Bondanella and Mark Musa (London: Viking Penguin, 1979), 48. In Italian original: Niccolò Machiavelli, *Arte della guerra e scritti politici minori*, ed.

Sergio Bertelli (Milan: Feltrinelli, 1961), 519: "Perché questa forma si può imprimere negli uomini semplici, rozzi e propri, non ne' maligni, male custoditi e forestieri. Né si troverà mai alcuno buono scultore che creda fare una bella statua d'un pezzo di marmo male abbozzato, ma sì bene d'uno rozzo."

37   Walter Benjamin, "The Work of Art in the Age of Its Reproducibility," in *Selected Writings, volume 3 (1935–1938)*, ed. Howard Eiland and Michael W. Jennings (Cambridge, MA: Belknap Press, 2002), 101–133, especially 121. This is the second version of Benjamin's essay, written in 1935–36, and published only posthumously.

38   *Mussolinis Gespräche mit Emil Ludwig, mit 8 Bildtafeln* (Berlin: Paul Zsolnay, 1932).

39   I am very grateful to Dan Sherer, who brought this image to my attention.

40   Gabriel Tarde, "What is a Sociology," in *The Laws of Imitation,* trans. Elsie Clews Parsons (New York: Henry Holt and Company, 1903), 78. Originally published as Gabriel Tarde, "Qu'est-ce qu'une société?" *Revue philosophique* 18 (1884): 489–510, especially 502: "Le magnetiseur n'a pas besoin de mentir pour être cru aveuglement par le magnétisé; il n'a pas besoin de terroriser pour être passivement obéi. Il est prestigieux, cela dit tout." See also Idem, *Les lois de l'imitation.* Étude sociologique (Paris: Alcan, 1890), 86. Tarde is mentioned in Le Bon, *Psychologie des foules*, 41: "un magistrat érudit, M. Tarde."

41   Gabriel Tarde, *Les Transformations du Pouvoir* (Paris: Alean, 1899), 25: "La vérité est que, pour la pluspart des hommes, il y a une douceur irrésistible inhérente à l'obéissance, à la crédulité, à la complaisance quasi-amoureuse à l'égard d'un maître admiré. C'est au fond ce que disait mon compatriote La Boëtie dans sa *Servitude volontaire.*" The reference to La Boëtie was brought to my attention by Annick Ohayon, "Entre Pavlov, Freud et Janet, itinéraire d'un gentilhomme russe émigré en France : Wladimir Drabovitch (1885–1943)," *Bulletin de psychologie* 521, no. 5 (2012): 479–85.

42   Tarde, *Les Transformations du Pouvoir*, 219–20: "Aussi pouvons-nous predire, à coup sûr, que l'Avenir verra des personifications de l'Autorité et du Pouvoir à côté desquelles pâliront les plus grandes

figures des despotes du passé, et César, et Louis XIV, et Napoléon
… cet homme d'Etat pourra réaliser des programmes politiques *et sociaux* d'une hardiesse qui aurait épouvanté Bismarck lui-même. Mais ce qui doit nous rassurer devant l'imminence de de 'Pouvoir gigantesque' c'est son élevation même."

43 See Le Bon, *Psychologie des foules*, 72 ff.: "Les meneurs de foules et leurs moyens de persuasion." Cf. De Felice, *Mussolini il rivoluzionario*, 462–64, 725–37, especially 736. In his introduction, Delio Cantimori stressed the importance of Gasti's report, xv–xvi.

44 See Andrea Cavalletti, *Suggestione. Potenza e limiti del fascino politico* (Torino: Bollati Boringhieri, 2011). The model for Thomas Mann's character was a well-known hypnotist, Cesare Gabrielli.

45 Michael Baxandall, *Painting and Experience in Fifteenth Century Italy. A Primer in the Social History of Pictorial Style* (Oxford: Clarendon Press, 1972).

46 Siegfried Kracauer, *From Caligari to Hitler: A Psychological History of German Film* [1947] (Princeton: Princeton University Press, 1973), 72–73.

47 See Sterling Fishman, "The Rise of Hitler as a Beer Hall Orator," *The Review of Politics* 26, no. 2 (1964): 244–256, especially 246, quoting Alfred Stein, "Adolph Hitler and Gustave Le Bon," *Geschichte in Wissenschaft und Unterricht* 6 (1955): 36 (which I have not seen).

48 Carsten Stage, "The Online Crowd: A Contradiction in Terms? On the Potentials of Gustave Le Bon's Crowd Psychology in an Analysis of Affective Blogging," *Distinktion: Scandinavian Journal of Social Theory* 14 (2013): 211–26, https://pure.au.dk/ws/files/54391668/OnlineCrowd_Stage.pdf.

49 See the passage quoted by Delio Cantimori, "Appunti sulla propaganda" [1941] in Idem, *Politica e storia contemporanea. Scritti 1927–1942*, ed. Luisa Mangoni (Torino: Einaudi, 1991), 685. See moreover Adolf Hitler, *Mein Kampf*, book I, ch. VI, trans. R. Manheim (Boston: Houghton Mifflin Company, 1943), 179–185: "All propaganda must be popular and its intellectual level must be adjusted to the most limited intelligence among those it is addressed to. Consequently, the greater the mass it is intended to reach, the lower its purely intellectual

level will have to be. ... The receptivity of the great masses is very limited, their intelligence is small, but their power of forgetting is enormous. In consequence of these facts, all effective propaganda must be limited to a very few points and must harp on these in slogans until the last member of the public understands what you want him to understand by your slogan. ... What, for example, would we say about a poster that was supposed to advertise a new soap and that described other soaps as 'good'? We would only shake our heads. Exactly the same applies to political advertising."

50   Le Bon, *Psychologie des foules*, 77: "De là la force étonnante de l'annonce. Quand nous avons lu cent fois, mille fois que le meilleur chocolat est le chocolat X, nous nous imaginons l'avoir entendu dire des bien des côtés, et nous finissons par en avoir la certitude."; Le Bon, *The Crowd*, 142.

51   Joseph Bédier, *Les crimes allemands d'après les témoignages allemands* (1915). I consulted the Italian translation: Joseph Bédier, *I crimini tedeschi provati con testimonianze tedesche*, trans. Antonio Rosa (Paris: Colin, 1915). See also Bédier and Bloch, *Storia psicologica della prima guerra mondiale*.

52   Carlo Ginzburg, "Lorenzo Valla on the 'Donation of Constantine'," in Idem, *History, Rhetoric, and Proof*, intr. Yosef Kaplan (Hanover, NH and London: University Press of New England, 1999), 54–70.

53   Carlo Ginzburg, "Anacronismi. Appunti su un equivoco," in *Ad placitum. Pour Irène Rosier-Catach*, vol. 1, ed. Laurent Cesalli, Frédéric Goubier, Anne Grondeux, Aurélien Robert, and Luisa Valente (Canterano: Aracne, 2021), 323–27.

54   Here I am quoting some passages from my essay "The Letter Kills. On Some Implications of 2 Corinthians 3:6," *History and Theory* 49 (2010): 71–89.

55   Lorenzo Valla, *De falso credita et ementita Constantini donatione declamatio* (*On the Donation of Constantine*) (Milan: Rizzoli, 1994), 56.

56   Leo Strauss, *Persecution and the Art of Writing* (New York: Free Press, 1952), 22–37.

129

Index

Ariosto, Ludovico, 2
Bataille, Georges, 57, 58, 59, 61–67, 70,
Baudelaire, Charles, 4, 36, 54
Bédier, Joseph, 94
Benjamin, Walter, 15–20, 26, 35–40, 58, 60, 83
Bloch, Marc, 71–73, 93
Boccioni, Umbert, 86–87
Caillois, Roger, 57–59, 64, 66
Châteubriant, Alphonse de, 64, 65
Clark, Kenneth, 27
Clastres, Pierre, 2,
de Maistre, Joseph Marie, comte, 43–54, 56–59, 64, 66, 67
Dreyfus, Alfred, 55, 56, 57,
Dürer, Albert, 24
Durkheim, Émile, 55–58
Evans-Pritchard, Edward, 56
Freud, Sigmund, 71, 78
Gutkind, Curt, 78–79
Halévy, Jacques Fromental, 40
Haskell, Francis, 20
Hitler, Adolf, 60, 62, 63, 78, 83, 89, 90, 93,
Hobbes, Thomas, 1–14
Joly, Maurice, 37, 38
Karr, Alphonse, 23–24
Klossowski, Pierre, 53, 54, 59, 60
Kojève, Alexander, 65, 70
La Boétie. Étienne, 1–14, 85
La Mennais, Félicité, 2

Laborde, Léon de, 20–40
Le Bon, Gustave, 73–78, 85, 86, 90–93
Lefebvre, Georges, 71, 73–74
Lefort, Claude, 13
Lefort, Claude, 2, 13
Leibniz, Gottfried Wilhelm, 42
Leopardi, 15
Leroux, Pierre, 3–7
Livy, 2, 49
Ludwig, Emil, 80, 81, 83,
Machiavelli, Niccolo, 38, 76, 80, 83
Mauss, Marcel, 55, 56, 58, 66
Merton, Robert K., 69–71, 73
Michelangelo, 30, 81, 82
Montaigne, Michel de, 1–4
Mussolini, Benito, 78–81, 83, 85, 86, 88
Nietzsche, Friedrich, 58, 62, 63
Pike, Kenneth, 26
Planche, Gustave, 20
Plato, 2, 5
Praz, Mario, 48
Pugin, Augustus Welby, 27, 28, 30
Queneau, Raymond, 64
Raoul-Rochette, Desiré, 33–34
Raphael, 15, 23, 24, 40
Rodrigues, Olinde, 6
Sade, Marquis de, 43, 44, 48, 49, 53, 54, 57, 58, 59, 62, 66, 67
Saint-Simon, Claude-Henri de, 4–6
Seneca, 2
Sieburg, Friedrich, 60
Sorbière, Samuel de, 7, 10
Stage, Carsten, 90
Tarde, Gabriel, 85, 86
Tolstoy, Leo, 45

132

Valla, Lorenzo, 94–96
Viollet-Leduc, Eugéne-Emmanuel, 32–34
Voltaire, 41–48, 51, 57, 73
Walpole, Horace, 27, 28
Weil, Simone, 2
Wiertz, Antoine, 36, 37, 39

www.ingramcontent.com/pod-product-compliance
Ingram Content Group UK Ltd.
Pitfield, Milton Keynes, MK11 3LW, UK
UKHW041402250225
455550UK00012B/36

9 789633 866412